Typical
American A$$hole

100 Ways
You Know
You are a TAA

Affan Ghaffari

Order this book online at www.trafford.com
or email orders@trafford.com

Most Trafford titles are also available at major online book retailers.

Printed in the United States of America.

ISBN: 978-1-4907-3869-7 (sc)
ISBN: 978-1-4907-3871-0 (hc)
ISBN: 978-1-4907-3870-3 (e)

Library of Congress Control Number: 2014910292

Trafford rev. 06/05/2014

 www.trafford.com

North America & international
toll-free: 1 888 232 4444 (USA & Canada)
fax: 812 355 4082

Acknowledgments

Many people inspired me to write this manuscript, but none of them want to be named due to the highly incendiary nature of this work so I have been told. However, you all know who you are and just remember I love you.

B ack in the Spring Semester at Florida State in 2007, I met Sharif who eventually became my best friend to the present day. Just like me, he is a Muslim, and we share the same conservative values in a campus that is as close to being conservative as Kim Kardashian is to being a nun. Let's just say that ship sailed far south several years ago. Whenever we witnessed the ubiquitous debauchery beleaguering FSU's campus while walking to and from class, Sharif would always remind me of a three-letter acronym coined by his father, which felicitously described these people. This three-letter acronym is simply expressed as TAA, which stands for typical American asshole. Thus, anytime we should head to the grocery store and see children acting like animals disrespecting their parents, we knew they were TAAs. Anytime we would see these salaciously dressed women (simply wearing their skimpy bikinis and panties as if they were dallying at a beach) lining up like slot machines in front of the Strozier Library, we knew they were TAAs. Anytime we would view a bunch of bibulous, puerile frat boys chugging down Heinekens like fish at 3:00 in the afternoon, we knew they were TAAs. Whenever we saw girls coming to class wearing their high heels, meager tissue-sized skirts shamelessly exposing their stomach and butt and provocative dresses unabashedly exposing their helium filled "balloobs" (inadequate boobs that need helium intervention in order to dilate like a balloon), we knew they were TAAs. I guess they were "dressing to impress" because I can assure you there was nothing impressive occurring at the top floor. Whenever we would head to the Taco Bell drive-thru, and they would predictably botch our order by either forgetting an item (typically my nachos and cheese) or forgetting to remove the beef from any of the items as I requested, we knew they were TAAs. Anytime we would head to a restaurant and we dealt with a snarky waiter who gauchely threw down his plates in disgust after a seemingly meager tip, we knew they were a TAA. Anytime we were on the road and some overzealous teenager failed to use a signal while cutting us off barely averting an accident, we knew they were a TAA. These experiences and a multitude of others have formed the underpinnings and inspiration upon which I write this book. It is time people actually realized how predictably and genuinely churlish, ignorant, overweening, and philistine Americans actually are despite the fact that people view America as the pinnacle of civilization. If this is the actual case, civilization has reprised in a "Dark Age." Now I want to share some of my wisdom on how you can actually spot a TAA (even inside of you) and just simply attribute the erratic behavior to those people to being TAAs. Here are one hundred ways (a) you can spot a TAA or (b) you know you are a TAA!

1. ***You find it acceptable to place your parents in a nursing home*** so your lazy princess ass does not have to take care of them at such a frail age. Certainly your parents did the same to you when they placed you in a nursery as a petulant and fractious child who would throw tantrums and whine when your parent would not buy you every toy in the store. Oh, that's right: they didn't.

2. ***You find it acceptable to elect a man into the Oval Office with no prior executive experience*** just because the quack on television told you to (Sorry, folks: I am not talking about the Aflac Duck as much as I am referring to Oprah "Winnie the Poof"-rey). I guess his looks didn't hurt either, did they, ladies? I guess the character Borat played in the namesake film accurately gauged the dangers of giving women the right to vote as akin to that of giving a monkey a gun. Obama sure possesses no qualms about women voting since his double-digit advantage amongst the female demographic in both elections fueled his election in 2008 and subsequent reelection bid in 2012. Congrats women: your superficial voting proclivities have contributed to the record-breaking increase of the federal deficit under Eating CrOw-bama as the deficit has already increased by over 6 trillion. Keep in mind the deficit increase under the not so curious George W. Bush only totaled $4.9 billion. You have to love the irony of the dual airbag Harvard graduates

teaming up to bankrupt the country over the last thirteen years. Makes you really question whether the best leaders get manufactured from Harvard or whether anyone teaches a useful course in economics there—you know one that edifies people on the dangers of deficit spending and superfluous bailouts. If only the Pills-buried Dough-Bama boy bailed out the Hostess Twinkies, many workers would not have been supplanted by machines under new ownership.

3. ***You find it acceptable to reelect a man who has failed*** to consummate any of his promises, increased the amount of people receiving food stamps by 70 percent, exacerbated the health care mess by introducing an abominable health care bill that is squeezing doctors and hospitals alike with no real cost control mechanisms in place, and continued to nourish the massive green giant known as the national debt with a $6 trillion (as of August 2013) increase during his presidency. I feel tempted to expound on Obama's ineptitude as a leader further, but it would require renaming this book "Jackass and the Beanstalk" since it involves a jackass (Obama) whose book of sins will take you up a perpetual giant green stalk to reach the end of it. Another potential parable inspired name for his abortive tenure as president would be PinocchiObama considering all his prevarications pertaining to the idea of "keeping your insurance if you like it." According to the Associated Press in December of 2013, 4.7 million cancellations of healthcare policies transpired due to Draconian Obamacare regulations which does not account for the losses in the small business health insurance market. I think what the Pillsbury Dough-bama boy meant to say is that if we like your health insurance, you can keep it because we the government know what's best for you. What do you call a government that brings it upon itself to decide what is best for its citizens without giving them the liberty to decide for themselves? Gosh, it stars with a "T" and it certainly fits the Obama administration to the "T." Alright, I will give Obama some credit for "ending" the American troops' involvement in Iraq in late 2011. However, that decision further exacerbated the plight of the country as

evident by Iraq's woefully high unemployment rates coupled by its persistent internal political strife neither of which the Obama administration cared to resolve. Thus, it still evinces a profound policy failure by a president who neglects to realize that leaving in the middle of the game does not scream heroism. Even if CroBama pulled the troops out of Iraq, does it really countenance his most egregious mushrooming prevarication pertaining to an individual's ability to retain their health insurance if they like it?

4. ***You fail to realize the real "conspiracy theory" behind 9/11 is the one promulgating the so-called Al-Qaeda group with their walkie-talkie phones somehow orchestrated a calculated attack on the Twin Towers and the Pentagon.*** Yet you neglected to ask for any evidence to back up this outlandish government claim; instead, you repudiate actual scientific evidence all pointing to an inside job as if the government has never deceived the public in the history of the United States. Did you ever ask yourself how a steel enforced building like the Twin Towers got brought down by fire when no steel enforced building in history has ever been brought down by fire alone? Keep in mind the head architect of the WTC (John Skillet) asserted the building as Boeing 707 proof and keep in mind the Boeing 707's size and fuel carrying capacity greatly exceeded that of the Boeing 767's that struck the tower. Have you ever asked yourself why there were heavy traces of superthermite at Ground Zero—the same characteristic material found at the sites of controlled demolitions? Have you ever wondered why Tower 7 fell even though it was not hit by any planes? Have you ever wondered why the prevaricating media unwittingly (and portentously) reported that Tower 7 collapsed even though the building stood erect in the background in plain sight? Have you wondered why the air force happened to hold its virtual emergency training the same day the planes got hijacked? Have you ever wondered why the tower that got hit later fell first? Have you ever wondered what happened to the indestructible black boxes of the two planes? Maybe the government wants to suppress your curiosity and pour a veil over your eyes to

obfuscate the fact they perpetrated this atrocity on their own citizens to justify going to war with Afghanistan and Iraq. The lack of intellectual curiosity and the obsequious willingness of the average American to accept anything the government says as fact formed the underpinnings for implementing an elaborate cover-up that could only dupe an obtuse American. I have spoken to educated people from India, China, Japan, Great Britain, and Canada and all these people laugh at the incredulity of Americans buying into the fallacious Hearst styled and McCarthyism inspired 9/11 Commission Report. The odious coverage of 9/11 from the American media proves that yellow journalism continues to persist and thrive even in the contemporary sophisticated technological age. As for the Pentagon saga, anyone that is fatuous enough to believe the government's version of a plane mysteriously swooping into the building and disappearing from the radar is not worth the oxygen they are breathing. Do you ever wonder why the 9/11 "investigators" ignored several hundred eyewitness testimony accounts? Do you ever wonder if was a coincidence that the part of the Pentagon being hit was the accounting department that could elucidate the unaccounted $3.1 trillion of defense spending promulgated by then Defense Secretary Donald Grumsfeld (forgive my incorrect spelling of his name to a name more appropriate of his demeanor) the day before? It's like all the idiots in this country who keep telling their children Santa Claus and the Tooth Fairy are real. In this case, the government is playing your role as the parents duping their incredulous children into believing an outrageous myth. Meanwhile, the government is surreptitiously force-feeding spurious information pertaining to the attacks into your anesthetized minds. In a way, it's better to be the children believing in Santa Claus because at least they get their desired gadgets and toys at the end of the day while the government gives you a combined $1.5 trillion bill on two fraudulent wars according to the National Priorities Project peeps (who have been nominated for a Nobel Peace Prize). Keep in mind not a single one of the arrogated attackers even came from Afghanistan or Iraq. Of course, when the Taliban asked for proof of Al-Qaeda involvement and the United States had none, they resorted to temper tantrums and war waging. And you wonder why we almost had a government shutdown and why the debt ceiling has to continue getting raised like the salaries of the CEOs at Goldman Sachs.

5. ***You lambaste and rebuke the radioactive effect of the Kardashians*** on the American culture/values (kind of an oxymoron if you ask me), yet you continue to tune in eagerly every Sunday (as well as Monday, Tuesday, Wednesday, Thursday, Friday, and Saturday when the E! network airs reruns of their show). Did it ever occur to you that your patronage of their sordid reality show is the reason why a) E! Network continues to air their show b) why they are so popular and rich and c) why your teenage daughters aspire to be like them due to the little effort they exerting in attaining their fame aside from the arduous hours of sex tape shooting and spreading their legs wider than the Amazon? I guess the Kardashians are living the true American dream after all—at least they are not robbing anyone in the process like Bernie Madoff. Oh wait a minute, they have robbed America of its masculinity (ask Kris Jenner where he has stored Bruce's man jewels) and its already dwindling moral compass. The Kardashian sisters have formed their own version of the KKK (Kim Khloe-rox Kourt-lan) on a mission to pulverize all semblance of values in America and convert all teenage girls to high-priced hookers one household at a time. Of course, charity begins at home as evident by their profound influence on their half-sisters Kendall (with her burgeoning modeling career on a quest to spreading her legs further and wider than any woman has ever gone) and Kylie (who has taken a page from the Kimberly playbook of hunting black male produce precociously through her budding romance with Will Smith's son). Now it seems as though Kendall and Kylie are racing to impress their eldest sisters by adding themselves to the "Unwed Mothers Club." My money is on the slightly more salacious Kylie who actually thought being a Jenner magically added five years to her age at a bar before being denied alcohol due to the fact that she is still five

years too young. She is what I term as a WCW (white crack whore) who will eventually become someone's "baby momma." So much for the desire to raise "traditional" girls, eh Kris?

6. ***You hurl otiose invectives at "illegal" Hispanic workers*** because you think they are stealing the jobs that you are unwilling to take anyway. Are you going to work in unsanitary construction projects in 100 degree weather? Are you going to clean and scrub the public toilets infested with feces and urine of people who obviously don't understand the concept of flushing the toilet or were never potty trained? Didn't think so. In one of the few encomiums I will deliver in this manuscript, the Hispanic workers you see in these contract and service positions are generally the most sedulous and honest people you will ever meet. They keep their heads down and do the work asked of them unlike most of the obnoxious white blonde bimbos you see in service positions who spend a lion's share of their time flirting with customers, texting, fixing their hair, or applying nail polish. If you want to discuss "parasites," look no further than regular Americans who complain about the work there not getting while performing meager work in the actual jobs they do obtain. Instead of sending more "illegals" back to Mexico or (insert Latin American county), we should send more Americans back to Europe to spruce their stagnant populations.

7. ***You fail to understand ESPN's agenda*** in their flagrantly biased (borderline hate speech) reporting of Tim Tebow as if he is the worst QB in NFL history just because he believes in God. Yeah, I understand Tim Tebow is not the most mechanically sound QB out there, but neither was Vince Young, JaMarcus Russell, Michael Vick, or Akili Smith. Yet, none of those guys were half as scrutinized or despised by the media as Tim Tebow despite the fact that Tebow has won the same number of playoff games as all those guys combined. Not to mention the fact that VY quit on his team on numerous occasions at Tennessee, JaMarcus Russell was an indolent bum who was 500 pounds overweight, and Michael Vick was a convicted dog killer (well technically he was convicted for operating the dog fighting ring, but I still see him as a dog

killer). You know I cannot be biased here when I am defending him not only as a Muslim, but as an FSU alum. Seriously, I have two superficial reasons to hate his guts, but I actually view him as a sacrificial lamb for a godless American media.

8. ***You fail to realize the double standard in the media's reporting*** of the Aurora theatre and Sandy Hood Elementary tragedies compared to the Boston Marathon "bombing"(these quotations have a deeper meaning). On one end, with the two white boys, they were "mentally disturbed" victims of bullying and a rampant "gun culture." Thus, society is partially responsible for their heinous actions. Over one and a half years have passed since the Aurora shooting and the trial starting date has yet to be materialized for the attacker. The reason centers on the sanity of the shooter James Eagen Holmes as he conveniently holds to the excuse of amnesia as a lame attempt to absolve himself of culpability. I think his hair should decide the sanity debate as he is dubbed the "Batman Killer" while he looks like a Joker. Instead of taking the socially painless route of overdosing (a la Heath Ledger), he decided to enact his fantasy on innocent patrons of a theatre. However, since Holmes was a budding academic luminary in the field of biology coming from an affluent Caucasian family, the media made it imperative upon themselves to formulate a de facto psych defense to construe his erratic behavior. As for the Sandy Hook child killer, the media was already armed with a built-in excuse in the form of the killer's gun loving mother. Her house contained enough of a gun repository to host a monogamous twenty-one gun salute for every fallen American soldier in Iraq for an entire year. Does anyone else find it stupefying (and perhaps a little equivocal) a kindergarten teacher harbored a gun infirmary in her house with a psychotic child in the house? Yeah, it's still the NRA's fault her son gunned down those kids. My personal favorite entailed the paltry media coverage surrounding the Fort Hood shooting when a former soldier killed three people and wounded sixteen more before ending his own life. The media and military establishment attributed this "unfortunate" behavior to PTSD—supposedly another

psychological disorder localized to white people and any other PC protected group such as the African Americans (cough cough Aaron Alexis the Navy Yard shooter) or the Yahudi.

On the other hand, the Chechen kid (arrogated as the Boston bomber) is depicted by the sagacious media as a typical Islamist, jihadist, terrorist who wants to indiscriminately murder Americans because surely all Muslims are terrorists deep inside while all white people are incredulous, pig-headed buffoons. Of course, there is no possibility of this kid suffering from a mental illness as well because apparently being born a Muslim is the most debilitating mental illness of all effectively obviating any alternative explanation of deviant behavior. The most harrowing aspect of the Chechen kid's ordeal concerns the lack of evidence to suggest his involvement in the "terror plot." Seems like he fits all the criteria of an Oswald (a.k.a. scapegoat) since the current criteria of being a terrorist consists of the following: being a Muslim, originating from a troubled part of the world composed primarily of Muslims, and being within five miles of the "terror zone" if the first two conditions are met. One vigilante powder keg Bostonian idiot chased down a Saudi national since he received Pavlovian conditioning training from the American media on how to spot a terrorist. It turned out the only crime the Saudi national committed entailed being a terrorist-looking Arab positioned within a few miles of the crime scene. Unfortunately, someone cannot get detained or imprisoned just because an invidious dope head feels uncomfortable about the presence of an Arab individual happening to walk the streets amidst a tumultuous situation. Thus, the Saudi national was released in the same pedestrian manner as the Muslims being blamed in the early stages of the 1994 Oklahoma City bombing before everyone ascertained that a white guy bombed children. Don't worry: it's only a matter of time before America categorically discards the Constitution and you can round up all the rag heads on your white horses.

9. ***You think a waiter/waitress at a restaurant deserves to get tipped 20 percent*** despite the fact they spent 80 percent of

the service playing with their cell phones tweeting about how much they hate their jobs. I never understood what was so "prompt" about checking in every twenty minutes and refilling drinks every thirty minutes. Maybe that's just my experience as a relatively corpulent and bearded Muslim terrorist plotting to institute the Sharia law in a country that is 0.2 percent Muslim. All joking aside, maybe they're just exasperated with the fact that I incessantly insist that all the entrees come without wine, pork or meat (since American meat slaughtering methods are both sordid and inhumane).

10. *You feel it is "chic" and fashionably sensible to buy ripped up jeans* at exorbitant prices from department stores. What next: are you going to buy a leftover hamburger that someone else partially ate, soup cans with torn off lids, bags of chips previously opened, a scratched laptop, a cracked big screen TV, or a prom dress vitiated with BBQ sauce—all at full price? Then again, males still line up to date the ultimate leftover piece of meat (Taylor Swift) containing bite marks from half the males in Dixieland. In America, leftovers certainly serve as the new fresh entrees.

11. *You actually think a toilet mounted on a wood desk or a stool with a basketball glued on top is "art"* and you glorify it in a museum as if it is a work of Da Vinci. Say what you want about the French, but they actually grasp the concept of art unlike Americans who think mass reproducing and reprinting art of great European artists is "art" in and of itself. Fucking Marcel Duchamp! On a serious note, when I visited my good friend Berry in Arkansas over Thanksgiving break in 2013, we decided to pay a visit to the prestigious Crystal Bridges Museum of American Art in Bentonville. The most staggering aspect of this visit entailed the ostensible dichotomy in the quality of American art in the eighteenth/nineteenth century and the "modern" period from the "Roaring Twenties" onward. Literally every piece of art in the "Modern" section fell under one or more of these qualities: recondite, prosaic, and harrowingly pathetic. Of course, the art snobs call it

"abstract" art, but I call it desultory shit. When I asked the so-called expert art curators in the establishment about what each of those pieces putatively symbolized, none of them could give me a lucid answer without having to consult a manger or even a handbook. Then they would try to convince themselves the title makes sense with specious arguments that neither Berry nor I bought for even a millisecond. Some of the most prominent examples of trashy art proudly displayed at this art institute are "Alphabets" by Jasper Johns, "Animal and Bird" by William Baziotes, "Black Balloon" by Gene Davis, "Center Column Blue and White" by Leon Polk Smith, "Chrysalis I" by Theodoros Stamos, "Cube" by Alvin Loving, "Coca Cola" by the magnate Andy Warhol, "Doros" by Theodoros Stamos, "Greek Tragedy" by Mark Rothko, "Man and Wife" by Milton Avery, "Homage to the Square" by Josef Albers, and "Reclining Women" by the beloved Jackson Pollock. Aside from the fact "Alphabets" did not contain anything resembling an alphabet, it appears someone vomited concrete from their system onto a canvas and whimsically called it art. As for "Animal and the Bird," it would have behooved the gentleman to take a zoology class to learn that a bird is an animal. Aside from the painter's ignorance about the Kingdom Animalia, there was nothing on the painting resembling an animal. In fact, it looked like a bird was unleashing its excretory contents on a sculpture of a chicken bone. "Black Balloon" forgot to include the balloon since it just included stripes of colors that had no business being lumped together. I will give the artist credit for having black stripes on his interpretation of the balloon. As for "Center Column Blue and White," it looked like someone with no ambition in life who decided to draw a desultory array of rectangles and squares to apply what little they learned in geometry. Aside from the fact they wanted to demonstrate their geometrical prowess, there was obviously no concrete message being purveyed through that painting. The purpose of any medium of artistic expression is to communicate your thoughts in a lucid manner. I guess this artist failed to learn that in second-grade English. As for "Chrysalis I," the artist should have named the painting "Crying for Cialis" because the painting was as tenebrous as the point he reached in his life with the dwindling testosterone levels. As for "Coca Cola," the painting literally exhibited a drawing of a pedestrian bottle of Coca Cola with the Coca Cola logo draped both on the bottle and separately to the side of the painting. The fact this blasé painting is considered "classic art" or even art in the first place seems to demonstrate America's infatuation with capitalistic motifs. Pretty soon, I will paint a Playtex tampon and a caricature of Lindsay Lohan as a subtle message advocating Lindsay Lohan (and only Lindsay Lohan) to utilize more contraception. That's all it would take to become the next Andy Warhol. Unlike Andy Warhol, my paintings will actually convey a concrete message of social awareness consisting of the necessity of preventing Lindsay Lohan from conceiving again not only to avoid another miscarriage, but to institute a societal quota for any more entitled spoiled bibulous towheads running around. As for "Cube" it literally shows a colored cube with squares cut into each of its faces. Clearly someone needed mommy to tell them they are special as a child. Clearly there is nothing special about being able to draw a cube. "Doros" should be renamed Dora the Explorer going inside a mule's ass because the painting literally looks like someone tied a stick to a rope around a mule and is scavenging through their ass. "Greek Tragedy" looks like someone who may have fantasized acting out a real life Greek tragedy called Oedipus as evident by the depiction of someone with a Goldilocks head covering wearing their mother's Red Wings themed bra along with their schoolgirl dress. Somehow the painting was supposed to reflect the horrors of World War II, but I guess the only horror from that painting resonates in the mind of the nutcase who painted it. "Man and Wife" seems to forget the wife unless the two faceless portraits in the background represent his wife. Or possibly he devoured his wife as the painting shows a guy with a petite face somehow possessing a waistline redolent of a pregnant woman wearing those stretchy Spandex pants. Either way, the painting is hideous. "Homage to the Square" evinces another example of a painter who loved geometry class a little too much as it depicts four concentric squares with a gradation in hue. The message of this painter seems similar to the message Cat Valentine (played by Ariana Grande in the popular Nickelodeon show "Sam and Cat") emphatically conveyed to Sam Puckett when she exclaimed "I know what I did, I take geometry!" Finally, "A Reclining Woman" seems to indicate the image of what a woman on LSD dreams about when reclining because it does not appear anyone is reclining amidst the dilapidated imagery presented in the painting. These paltry quality paintings seem to illustrate America's diluting standards in what constitutes legitimate art and furthermore growing appreciation of the disjointed, mediocre and pedestrian. Americans have forgotten that art too represents a profound medium of communication requiring a meaningful purpose. However, the growing emphasis on nihilism and "cultural relativism" in America reflects in its floundering appreciation for the arts along with the vitiation of the core meaning of art. Not surprisingly, when Berry and I left the museum, we spoke to a Betty and Billy Bob couple in the elevator who seemed to think all the paintings in the museum were "amazing" as if they have been preprogrammed to think that every painting which makes it into a museum automatically qualifies as a "masterpiece." Clearly Americans have lost their sense of reality when it comes to critically examining art as well as descrying sophisticated art from the philistine.

12. ***You are unable to find Iraq on a map*** even though American troops had spent nearly a decade molesting that country for every last drop of oil they have while failing to quell tensions between Sunni and Shi'ite as Saddam did so efficiently the previous twenty-plus years. Seriously, according to the National Geographic Society, 63 percent of Americans could not find Iraq on a map. Thus, 63 percent of Americans don't know where $1.7 trillion of their tax dollars have gone over the last decade.

13. ***You cannot find Afghanistan on a map*** despite the fact the "War on Terror" started there since all those hijackers who crashed the Boeings into the Twin Towers came from

Afghanistan (actually none of them did, but we are supposed to believe the Taliban sent them like we believe vehemently in the Tooth Fairy and Santa Claus). According to the same report mentioned in my previous point, 90 percent of respondents could not locate Afghanistan on a map. I am sure there is an app for that, right Android and Apple?

14. ***You pronounce Iran as "I ran,"*** which is a lie in and of itself since two out of three Americans are overweight or obese according to the National Institute of Health possibly because they are anorexic to any form of physical activity. The only "running" Americans seem to do is from the truth that America and "I ran" are more alike than anyone in Washington would like to admit.

15. ***You pronounce Iraq as "I rack"*** as if you are talking about a speeding ticket you racked up or the incessant pool of educational debt you have been swimming in since you cannot seem to find a decent paying job despite possessing a Bachelor's (and in some cases a Master's degree). Seems like America should just rename Operation Freedom as "I Rack" as well because they have done nothing but rack up billions of dollars of debt themselves in the country of "I Rack."

16. ***You still think Lee Harvey Oswald killed JFK*** despite the fact that Lee Harvey Oswald was behind him and JFK's head jerked back and to the left. Common sense physics suggests that if the momentum stemming from a bullet thrusts someone's head backward, the bullet came in front of them. That coupled with the eyewitness accounts of noise from the so-called Grassy Knoll indicate the shooter was in that area rather than a covered building as asininely purported. Of course, the US government never lies in their "official" reports. It's also not a coincidence that all the main players involved in the conspiracy (LBJ, Nixon, Ford, and Bush Sr.) all became US presidents bound by the secret encompassing the plot to kill JFK. JFK was killed in LBJ's backyard while LBJ proceeded to plagiarize all of JFK's ideas under the guise of the "Great Society." As for Nixon

and Bush Sr., the fact there is video footage of them in Dallas on the same day they conveniently forgot their whereabouts negates their credibility. Not to mention HW worked for the CIA who wanted nothing more than to eliminate a president who was punching holes in their insidious plans. As for the charity case Gerald Ford, it's shady enough he headed the specious Warren Commission and became part of the first non-elected President/VP duo in American history. However, did anyone ever wonder why he pardoned Nixon? Could it relate to the fact that Nixon possessed the ability to bring down the house of cards that was the JFK murder plot? As the Nixon character played by Anthony Hopkins said in the namesake film "I know enough about this country to destroy it." There lied a profound deeper meaning to that quote more than most Americans will ever realize.

17. ***You watch the hit MTV show "16 and Pregnant"*** with such keen interest and amusement yet fail to understand how this show is promoting a repugnant culture of salaciousness and diffuse responsibility amongst teenagers. Their situation is not "amusing" when you consider the burden of their "unwanted" pregnancies and concomitant costs relating to the baby falls on the taxpayers—$10.9 billion annually according to the National Campaign to Prevent Teen and Unplanned Pregnancy. Think about that next time you don't want to edify your teenagers about the arcane concepts of abstinence and contraception instead opting to expose them to the trashy sluts on "16 and Pregnant" who are busy telling them how to get famous by spreading their legs a little more.

18. ***You pronounce Islam with a z rather than an s.*** I guess this is the American way of pandering to the Japanese (who confuse their L's with R's) or even Indians from the subcontinent (who confuse their B's with V's). Now it's time to kiss your significant other under the mizzletoe during Chrizmaz. Another example of Americans confusing the z and s is evident when pronouncing Muslims as "Moz-lems" as in "Mozlems killed us on 9/11" as uttered by Bill O'Reilly once on "The

17

View." Then again, it is possible "Mozlems" refer to some elitist secret society or sect of the Free Masons who are responsible for all the evil in America anyway. However, my bet is that the term "Mozlems" represent the dimwitted and slipshod attempt by Americans to pronounce Muslims correctly kind of like a little child who struggles to pronounce words like "marathon," "yellow," or "strawberry" correctly. In the case of children, the mispronunciations serve as a source of cloying moments. However, when adults resort to mispronouncing simple words, it is redolent of a nuisance since adults should not be as inept as toddlers in speech. As the meddling character Marie from "Everyone Loves Raymond" said to her Frankenstein of a son when he precipitously decided to receive Botox injections thereby hindering his speech "Robert, please stop talking like that dear. It's really annoying." My other favorite entails American confusion of the letters k and q. This is particularly evident in their egregiously inaccurate pronunciation of the Islamic holy text Qur'an (not Koran). Enunciate it Americans: it starts with a Q not a K.

19. ***You actually believe Jesus' birthday was on December 25.*** I don't know of any shepherd who is tending and watching their flock during frigid weather conditions in December. Not to mention the Bible itself (specifically Luke 2:1–4) mentioned the decree of a census ordered by Caesar Augustus around the time of Jesus' birth. As history (and good old-fashioned common sense) would suggest, the census is conducted anytime between spring and fall during ideal weather conditions and not during the frosty conditions of December in Bethlehem. Thus, the evidence presented in the Bible itself of the shepherd tending their flock and the census being conducted both contradicts the asinine bedtime story of Jesus being born in December. It would be better if you all just admitted that you are pagans at heart and you use this "holiday" as an excuse to engage in prodigal spending to drive up your credit card debt en route to eventual bankruptcy and credit dissolution. Of course you will be delusional enough to convince yourself the smile on your son (or daughter or transvestite)'s face while buying him the new

X-box system was worth all these financial headaches. News flash: the half-life of gaming consoles in the status quo is like one year. Give yourself a pat on the back for refined parenting skills when your child swindles another game system out of you the next year and the year after that.

Even more egregious than the fact Americans celebrate Jesus' birthday on the wrong day entails their predilection with wearing the cross. Let's pretend for a minute that Jesus was actually crucified on a cross (which I repudiate as a Muslim), I fail to understand the logic of carrying around the symbol pertaining to his painful death. It is analogous to African Americans carrying around a bullet of MLK Jr. to commemorate the fact he got shot to death or Indians carrying around a necklace containing a knife symbolizing the perfidious act of Mahatma Gandhi's own bodyguard gunning him down. Better yet, why don't people wear chains of mini beer bottles to commemorate the fact their family member was killed by a drunk driver? When I have discussed this with many Christians, they cannot provide a concrete explanation to justify their dastardly behavior aside from the whole "You can't understand because you're not Christian" bromide. As a retort, I would pull a page from celebrity chef Gordon Ramsay to a haughty Frewish Jewrench (hybrid French and Jew) chef after hearing his explanation for unwittingly freezing oysters. Ramsay exclaimed "I'm just trying to get inside your mind to break down how stupid you are." Apparently being Jew could not save him from the air headedness associated with being French just like an Oxford education cannot save a Christian from their perpetual wayward logic.

20. ***You fail to acknowledge the term "Indian" to describe Christopher Columbus was actually a misnomer in itself*** since the jackass confused the natives with actual Indians from the subcontinent. Well over five centuries later, we are continuing this jackass tradition by falsely imputing the term "Indian" to Native Americans. Perhaps the national animal for America should be the donkey rather than the bald eagle. Not to mention the fact America celebrates

Columbus with a national holiday—the same Columbus who ruthlessly enslaved and subjected Indians to Draconian working conditions forming the underpinnings for the slavery movement in the United States. If a Native American enslaving murderer like Columbus is a hero, we should devote a holiday commemorating Andrew Jackson for his outstanding work during the "Trail of Tears." In all honesty, one can argue Andrew Jackson was one of the more charismatic and momentous figures in American history when you consider his contributions during the War of 1812 (specifically the Battle of New Orleans) as well as his instrumental role in the United States seizing control of Florida in subsequent years. Not to mention the fact he revolutionized the US presidency with his "spoils system" as well as being the first common man ever to ascend to the post. The fact that we as a country condone Columbus' treatment of Indians and vilify Andrew Jackson for his similar treatment of Indians illustrates a harrowing double standard in our society's interpretation of history. America seems to feed on double standards making it the land of the hypocrisy and the home of the deprave-d.

21. *You feel the need to measure everything in pounds, gallons, and feet* just to be different from the rest of the world. The SI system was designed for simplicity purposes so the mathematically inept Americans can competently record and interconvert data instead of generating arbitrary units of measurement to further flabbergast themselves. Now all we have done is given our overworked high school students more difficult conversion problems in chemistry. How do you expect a student to memorize there are 3.785 Liters in a gallon or 2.2 pounds in a kilogram? Even the whole length conversion process is dilapidated since you start with 12 inches equaling 1 foot and then 3 feet equaling 1 yard. Clearly the American metric system boasts of as much consistency throughout the conversion process as a twister (and not the Jennette McCurdy and Andre Drummond version).

22. *When you are in high school and you still use your hands and long multiplication to solve math problems* rather than

your brain. Perhaps if Americans used their brains more for easy calculations, they could catch up to the other twenty-four industrialized nations that are kicking their butts in math. The sad part about the OECD study is that it only included twenty-seven industrialized countries. I wonder what kind of outrage would ensue if America finished twenty-fifth out of those same twenty-seven industrialized countries in medal count at the Summer Olympics or in the World Basketball Championship. Take home message: it's okay to be dumber than them as long as we are faster and stronger. Do they still teach the parable of the hare and the tortoise in American schools?

23. *You sit inside a movie theatre posting on your Facebook wall* how exciting the new Batman (or Superman or Spiderman or other hackneyed and recycled superhero series) movie is, taking a pic on your smartphone of the wonderful time you are having with your "significant other (s)," posting the pic on Instagram, and then Tweeting to the entire world that you are at the movie theatre watching Batman with your significant other. Whatever happened to the concept of "Silence is golden" inside a movie theatre or even the idea of "spending a quality intimate night out"? I guess the cell phone has become our puppet dictator or the obnoxious mother in law that wants to accompany you on the honeymoon.

24. *You are willing to spend two hours, $3 on a small drink, $5 on medium popcorn, and $50 for four tickets at a movie theatre every week*—all of which catalyze your journey to tooth decay and profound chronic illnesses. Yet you throw a fit about a $10 copay to your primary care doctor or the $50 to your dentist—both of whom are trying to prevent you from getting those illnesses. Guess math and common sense are not American specialties after all.

25. *You spend at least $100 on a family dinner each week at Longhorn Steakhouse* when that same $100 could buy you two weeks' worth of food at the local grocery stores (Okay, maybe one week of food in New York or Massachusetts). Gee,

would I rather be adequately fed for two hours or two weeks? Would I rather eat food that clogs my arteries or food that my body can actually digest properly without being manifested in body fat? Gosh, the choices are so tough here. Can I use the 50/50?

26. ***You complain about your child's bill after their visit to the orthodontist or pediatrician*** yet you gleefully spend twice as much for your dogs at a veterinarian. Fact: Americans spend $18 billion on their pets' medical services to the point where our nation is seriously advocating health insurance for pets. Wake up America: cats and dogs are not people.

27. ***You eagerly purchase alcoholic beverages at sporting events despite bringing your kids*** to the game. Then you get drunk, loud, and obnoxious at the game—once again neglecting to note there are kids around. Afterward, you are genuinely amazed a couple of years later when your teenagers are acting boisterous and binging on alcohol. This is what my friend Sharif and I refer to as "TAA training." In most American households, it initiates earlier than toilet training.

28. ***You deem it appropriate to smoke in public*** and expose other people to second hand smoke. It's your right to expose yourself to seventy carcinogenic chemicals while smoking. However, who gave you the right to expose hundreds of thousands of other people to bronchitis, heart disease, and lung cancer? According to the US Department of Health and Human Services, second hand smoke is responsible for 150,000–300,000 new cases of bronchitis and pneumonia yearly in children eighteen months or younger along with 7,500–15,000 hospitalizations annually in the same age group. I could cite a plethora of statistics on the pernicious effects surrounding second hand smoke, but the aforementioned statistics for toddlers should precipitate enough of a stomach churning effect for the idiots shamelessly smoking in public areas. That's the beauty of living in an "individualistic" American society: it obviates the need to give a fuck about anyone else. Score

another round for Western philosophy. Meanwhile, more children continue to get afflicted with asthma—sometimes lacking the necessary access to corticosteroids.

29. ***You let your daughters (as young as three years of age) roam around in public wearing skimpy clothing*** exposing their backs, chests, and everything below their knees. Yet you develop this dubious expectation they will learn modesty by the time they are teenagers when you have been dressing them with an ostensible lack of modesty. This underscores another profound example of the term "TAA training." Now you wonder why so many middle aged men are becoming pedophiles these days with all the skin being exposed on the backs of little girls being dressed by their equally slutty mothers.

30. ***You complain about Wal-Mart and their unscrupulous practices in relation to their labor and exploitation of cheap markets.*** On the other hand, you mirthfully shop there to save a few extra bucks a week and tout Wal-Mart Visitor Center Museum as an "historical landmark." Sounds like the typical Rachel Green (from the '90s hit show "Friends") petal plucking dance between "I hate Ross" and "I love Ross." Predictably, Wal-Mart loves you since they are the only ones who ever seem to flourish even in an economic downturn. However, I must say the Walton family possesses a sick sense of humor in their glorification of a particular Jewish family in early America named Levy-Franks. As told in their description of the six family portraits of the Levy-Franks clan proudly displayed in the Crystal Bridges museum owned by the Walton family, "the Levy Franks family held a prominent place in New York's Jewish and mercantile communities." Of course, the museum bowdlerizes the fact this same Levy-Franks family were responsible for overseeing the development of the ships that brought in slaves from Africa during the time of the Atlantic Triangular Slave Trade. On the way across the Atlantic, one-third of the slaves died as a result of the besmirched and grisly conditions upon which they were

transported while one-third of the slaves transported were of Muslim origin. Quite fitting that a Jewish family find themselves profiting off the humiliation of Muslims as if that does not transpire on a quotidian basis along the Gaza Strip and West Bank. Americans are too ignorant to realize the top three slave trading states in America were all up north—Rhode Island, Massachusetts, and Connecticut. Families such as the Levy-Franks brigade brokered the slave trade and profited immensely from the intransigent labor and profound human rights abuses imposed on African Americans during that time. Wal-Mart chooses to commemorate the benevolent, puritanical, and virtuous Levy-Franks family during the most titillating time in American history when Africans were bounded by dog collars onto ships and forced into chattel slavery in the states. I guess the Walton family and this Levy-Franks clan share some ostensible traits such as the indefatigable pursuit of money and the callousness toward human life encrusted in their belief equating workers with machines. Then again, the Waltons must feel the pressing need to honor the underlying American belief that all Jews walk on water and no deed from a Jew is too small, especially the Jews who are responsible for bringing all those savages from Africa on ships so they could plow our fields and build our railroads. Maybe the Walton family should consider buying all the family portraits of the Capones, the Rosenbergs, and Frank Lucas's family as well due to the profound impact from each of these families on American society and concomitant culture. Then the Waltons can assiduously demonstrate the fact they appreciate scumbags of all races and ethnicities, not just the water-walking Jews.

31. ***You sport a sententious façade (to the point of being bathetic) concerning any outward display of Anti-Semitism,*** but you have no qualms patronizing a company (Ford) whose founder (Henry Ford) was unabashedly anti-Semite. I am guessing the Ford Museum neglected to display exhibits germane to his newspaper titled *The Dearborn Independent* in which he promulgated the idea of a vast Jewish conspiracy pervading America. Nor will you find the compilation of his

articles pertaining to the "infectious" Jews in an anthology titled "The International Jew" of which he disseminated over half a million copies across all of his dealerships and subscribers with the same verve Planned Parenthood distribute condoms to high schools across the country. On top of touting Ford as the paradigm American car company, Henry Ford is viewed as a visionary, a pioneer, and a genuine American hero. I think it's time to give Prescott Bush and Mel Gibson the same kind of love, don't ya think? Then again, it would not really matter if the Jews knew of Henry Ford's animus toward them because Ford cars lack the luxuriousness Jews yearn in a car anyway since they typically prefer Mercedes or another upscale company. Somehow Obama is considered an anti-Semite to many in the media ranks even though he has diverted more public funds toward the Israeli military than any other president in US history. Not to mention the blockade he has instituted against any potential challenge the UN has wanted to levy against Israeli for their shamelessly illegal squatter settlements in the Gaza Strip and West Bank. Basically, America vehemently opposes apartheid unless Israel is the one instituting it as they are callously doing in their illegal occupation of the aforementioned areas. In short, America has become Israel's "pimp daddy" to the point where they have preemptively bought $2 billion of the V-22 Osprey planes on a "deferred payment plan" in early April 2014. Danny Ayalon (former Israeli ambassador to the US) promulgated it was plausible for the Israeli government to anticipate extension of the foreign military aid due to widespread congressional support for the Jewish State. That is politician speak citing the fact that the United States government will bow down to the wishes of their fiendish ventriloquist. Perhaps the United States should consider a name change to become the United Snakes of America kowtowing to the desires of the ultimate serpent in Israel. Maybe the liberals had it correct when vociferously advocating for the words "Under God" to be stricken from the Pledge of Allegiance. Perhaps they should supplant the words "Under God" with "Under Israel's ass" to accurately reflect the tendentious nature of America's foreign policy. It is disgraceful for an effete United Snakes of America to arrogate itself as "one nation under God" when they categorically support a rogue state like Israel responsible for levying the most flagrant human rights abuses in the world today through a ruthless and sadistic apartheid campaign against those in the Gaza Strip and West Bank. It seems like America forgot what it was like to get snake bitten by their perfidious Israeli friends in the USS *Liberty* incident when the Israeli jet fighter planes and torpedo boats viciously attacked a US Navy technical research ship killing thirty-four crew members and injuring another 171. Israel claims it was a case of mistaken identity for an Egyptian ship even though the US *Liberty* was twice the size of the putative Egyptian vessel, contained Roman lettering instead of Arabic lettering, and clearly displayed the US flag. The credibility of Israel is further compromised by the testimony of USS *Liberty* crew members indicating that Israeli planes were flying over the vessel in intervals at low altitudes before eventually assailing it. Of course, the US government has become inveterate to giving its ventriloquist blow jobs to the extent they are willing to countenance a blatant and sinister attack on their own naval service members to continue their skewed policy of favoritism. In the spirit of commemorating the United States service to Israel, I will await a notice from the Anti-Defamation League lapdogs citing this book for "Anti-Semitism" in their ineluctable quest to prove their fealty to their masters at the AIPAC.

32. ***You conveniently summon your first amendment rights for freedom of speech*** yet you completely ignore that same first amendment concerning freedom of religion when vitriolically attempting to sabotage the development of a mosque in places like NYC, Boston, and Murfreesboro (TN). Of course, you conjure tenuous arguments such as the mosque being a "front for terrorism" as if Islam is the only religion with zealots. Yet there is no outrage for the development of a Catholic cathedral despite the strong connection between Catholic priests and pedophilia to the extent the US Roman Catholic Church has paid out $3 billion in "hush money" settlements over the past two decades to the parents of molested children. Thankfully

this has resulted in the closure of eight diocese branches due to bankruptcy. In a way, America is slowly disinfecting itself of the pestilence that is Catholicism.

33. ***You feel the need to utilize the hash tag (#) at the end of all your tweets*** and wall postings to summarize your thoughts of someone, something, or some situation. #Lame #Hypocritical #Ignorant #Vapid. Okay, now I am getting hash tag happy in describing what I feel about most Americans. I have reached my hash tag quota for this century. Maybe I will just channel that energy to making tic-tac-toe boards and playing Cat's games on Valentine's Day with Ariana Grande on the Way to being Victorious over my Problem.

34. ***You find the act of wasting food at a restaurant indicative of a lofty "status symbol"*** regardless of the profound effort it took from people working at a pittance to cook and serve the food. Not to mention the fact that 3.5 million children around the world die of malnutrition. Furthermore, 870 million (1/8 of the world) suffer from chronic undernourishment annually. According to the most recent USDA and EPA estimations (2010), around 133 billion pounds of food from US retail food stores, restaurants, and homes failed to reach the rapidly expanding American stomachs. The EPA also reported that food waste constituted the greatest portion of waste entering landfills as Americans callously waste 40 percent of their food. I can understand why people waste food in a restaurant if they genuinely find it inedible. If that were the case, it would be more salubrious just to call your server to properly toss the rancid food and tell them how to improve the quality. Instead, many Americans simply leave plates teeming with food on the table without any regard for their own money, the chefs/cooks who travailed in making the food or the millions of Americans on food stamps who would kill for the opportunity to munch on restaurant quality food. Perhaps you should lay low on the bread or other starches that prevent you from being able to fit that 12 ounce medium rare prime rib steak into your turgid pouch. Or perhaps you should learn the concept of putting the leftover food in a box to prevent yourself from looking like a wastrel pig. Then

again, wasting food under the guise of flaunting your wealth also works.

35. ***You refer to your sports teams who win league championships as "world" champs.*** Last time I checked, all the teams in the MLB, NBA, NFL, and NHL are located in North America. Since when did conquering North America become equivalent to conquering the world? I guess the au courant American view of geography is that America is the world based on the fact most of Americans could not name five countries outside the North American continent. Wait a minute; most Americans cannot name five countries within the North American continent either. Heck, Taylor Swift probably could not name five US states without consulting the tour calendar on her iPhone listing all the guys she screwed in the different states of her tour.

36. ***You gleefully eat the Fried Cheese Melt at Denny's*** even though it is literally a heart attack on a plate with four cheese sticks and melted American cheese crunched between two slices of sourdough bread. The French don't even eat that much cheese in a week. Maybe Steve Urkel should have waited another decade and a half to go off air so he could enjoy his own mini cheese bar on a plate at Denny's.

37. ***You have a penchant for putting bacon on everything*** from pancakes to candy canes to shaving cream to milkshakes (looking at you Jack in the Box) to cologne (thanks to Fargginay), to soda to vodka to bandages to toothpaste (courtesy of Mr. Bacon). Apparently the saying "you are what you eat" is not broad enough to describe Americans. It should be "you are what you eat, drink, wear, shave, and spray." With the average American consuming fifty-one pounds of pork in a year, it has become obvious how the pork has permeated deeply into the brains of Americans as well to the point where they will eventually start breathing through pork-based tubes.

38. ***You drench your daily "healthy" salad with blue cheese dressing, ranch dressing, bacon, and chicken*** and are still

surprised that you are not losing weight. News flash: there are more calories in your "salad" than a Quarter Pounder combo at McDonalds. Those calorie counts the restaurants give on the salad are sans any condiments or meat items. Also, the fact your salad contains "processed" fruits and vegetables lathered with pesticides and carcinogenic additives does not help either.

39. ***You feel the need to celebrate and commercialize a "holiday" like Halloween*** despite its ostensible connections to witchcraft, voodoo and Satanic worship. Then you further vitiate it by using it as an excuse for your kids to beg neighborhoods across the town for candy to drive your all out "candy binge." As if it is not enough for 42 percent of American children between the ages of two and eleven dealing with tooth decay in their primary teeth. Now you compound the issue by encouraging them to engage in the frivolous behavior of excessive candy eating which evinces one of the main culprits causing tooth decay in children. Go figure these are probably the same parents who allow their high school children to throw keg parties. I'm not advocating for an abrogation of candy by any stretch, but we should also not commercialize holidays that encourage incessant candy stuffing.

40. ***You follow the GPS as religiously as Ron Burgandy read off the teleprompter*** (if you did not watch the movie "Legend of Ron Burgandy" with Will Ferrell, you will not understand this reference) to the point you will do anything and I mean anything the GPS tells you to do. Even if that means turn right on Vista Point 166 and send your car flying off the cliff. Will do. Make an illegal turn left on the intersection into oncoming traffic. Will do. Take the highlighted route that will lead to exorbitant fees stemming from tolls instead of the route that will allow you to dodge tolls and get you there at the same time. Will do. News flash America: the GPS is not God and there are times where it does not show you the quickest route. Instead, the GPS sometimes shows you the "shortest" route which requires excursions into hillbilly land that end up taking two hours than the other routes. True story: when I visited my

friend Berry in Arkansas during Thanksgiving break in 2013, I used the lovely TomTom GPS, which I received at a hefty discount online at Bestbuy.com. The GPS possessed many neat features including the efficient search engine and the speed limit indicator. However, the route they gave me involved toll roads in the Indian Reservation Territory in Oklahoma. Not only did this antediluvian toll road accept credit cards as payment, but it took me about a half an hour longer to reach my destination than it would have if it just showed me the route through Dallas from College Station. On the way back, I learned my lesson by eschewing the toll road in favor of the road leading to Dallas. Consequently, my estimated arrival time (ETA) decreased appreciably. At this point in time, I realized the "fastest route" option on my GPS does not actually apply in the presence of toll roads since these GPS companies likely have deals with the toll companies. Notice none of the GPS companies readily give you the non-toll routes. When dealing with the possibility of a toll route, never trust the GPS and use your good old fashioned common sense.

41. ***You blame the officiating or the weather every single time your team loses.*** Living in Boston for close to three years, I became inured to their excuses as to why their teams lost and most of them dealt with the refs or the weather. Do you understand that refs could face time in a federal prison if they fixed games in one team's favor? Do you honestly think they would risk going to prison so they could make your team lose? Yes, there are games where the officiating is abysmal, but generally that affects both teams. As for the weather excuse, I am pretty certain both teams were playing in the same snow and rain. The better team is able to adjust to those hardy conditions and win. Just deal with the fact your team is not as good as you thought they were. In the case of Bostonians, I doubt the possibility of their team ever being as superlative as the delusional Bostonians think. Case closed. True story: one of my good friends in Boston actually thinks the Patriots would have destroyed the Seahawks in the Super Bowl despite the fact the Patriots got emasculated by the same Broncos team that got

castrated by the Seahawks. Sorry Bostonians: football does not work like rock, paper, and scissors.

42. ***You were quick to verbally crucify the jury in the OJ Simpson case*** because he was obviously guilty of murdering his ex-wife and her boyfriend. If OJ Simpson was guilty, could you kindly explain why there were no defensive wounds or traces of blood spatter on his body or clothing when they strip searched him later that night in the LA police precinct? I guess OJ is such a badass that his ex-wife and her martial arts trained beau would just bow down to him and let him stab them to death without putting up a fight. How about OJ's son (Jason) who actually had a history of blowing his fuse prompting the doctors to put him on Depakote to deal with his "intermittent rage disorder"? Keep in mind Jason had the history of using deadly weapons to threaten the likes of his girlfriend and boss. Also keep in mind Jason son was off his medication for two months prior to the night in question. Not to mention the fact that Nicole and Ronald were supposed to dine in that night at the restaurant Jason worked, but reneged on this promise. Furthermore, Jason handwrote his clock out time despite the fact the restaurant had a computerized system that was working the night in question. Most of all, the ligature indention patterns of the knife made on Nicole's skull matches the knife found in Jason's storage locker several years later. This case illustrated two points: (1) how racist, short-sighted, and obtuse the LAPD has always been and (2) how the American public seems to dance to the tunes of the biased American media. In short, OJ was not guilty in 1994 just like Oswald was not guilty in 1963.

43. ***You vilify PED and steroid users*** as if you never cheat in your daily lives. People like Lance Armstrong, Marion Jones, Barry Bonds, Mark McGwire, and Ryan Braun are pariahs just because they did something most other Americans would do in the same situation. According to Business News Daily, one-third of Americans admit to cheating on their timesheets. Thus, you are earning money for work you did not even perform

and effort you did not invest. According to Pew Research on Tax Foundation, 1.6 million Americans cheat on their taxes annually to swindle the government of money that could be allocated to more deserving people or processes. At the end of the day, who did these athletes really cheat except for themselves and a few overzealous fans who have nothing better to do with their pathetic lives aside from living vicariously through their beloved athletes? As for your kids in college, 75–98 percent of them admit to cheating at some point during their academic careers. Let's make all these people pariahs as well. Pretty soon, everyone will be an outcast except for the liars who don't admit to cheating at any point of their lives. Please discard the double standard America! Your athletes are human just like you and me.

44.   To expatiate upon my previous point, *you abhor cheaters in sports more than actual cheaters in real life when it comes to marriage vows.* The list I formulated earlier of PED users evinced some prominent names. However, they pale in comparison to the likes of Kobe Bryant, Magic Johnson, Michael Jordan, Tiger Woods, Rick Pitino, Larry Bird, and Dan Marino—all of whom committed adultery at one point during their playing or coaching careers. Yet all of them are touted as heroes, legends, Hall of Famers, and luminaries in their respective sports. Basically, this means we as a society give greater weight to our sports competitions than our marriages. Apparently, as long as you are winning championships and breaking records, Americans really do not care about the emotional/psychological damage you may cause to your significant other as well as your children. But how dare you betray our trust by using PEDs because we really believed a skinny thirty home run hitting man could naturally evolve into a surly seventy home run hitting monster particularly after he crossed thirty years of age? Moreover, I find it kind of comical that we as a society sympathize with Magic Johnson and his HIV struggle when it is clear his promiscuous behavior caused it. Could it have to do with our strained priorities as a society giving athletes a pass on anything sans the "cardinal sin" of using PEDs?

45. ***You think the proverbial "friends with benefits" arrangement can actually work.*** Here's the catch (aside from the occasional herpes): women produce a hormone during sex called oxytocin which generates a potent emotional connection. Thus, no matter how diligently women try to convince you otherwise, they will always develop some kind of emotional connection as a result of having sex with you. Sorry, it's not a sexist comment: it's just science. Thus, it's nearly impossible to have sex with a woman and remain "just friends" because feelings will develop inevitably on the female side. Plus, the only benefit men will ever get in any relationship with a woman is the six letter V word while everything else that accompanies a woman is a side effect. With some drugs, the benefit may not be worth the side effects. Ask Kris Humphries, Miles Austin, or Reggie Bush.

46. ***You blame the "video game culture"*** for the brutal violence occurring in public schools as well as in America altogether. Here are some statistics: 97 percent of teens play video games, two thirds of males play video games with an *M* rating while one fourth of girls play video games (including Morgan Webb) with the *M* rating. It does not take a gargantuan study to understand that 97 percent of teens are not committing crimes or engaging in school shootings. Furthermore, two thirds of teenage boys are not carrying guns and knives to school hacking old women crossing the street like they do in those "Grand Theft Auto" games. According to a 2007 study from the Journal of Adolescent Health (a reliable source unlike all the pompous gun control advocates like Bob Costas), video games serve a salubrious purpose in potentially averting crime as 45 percent of boys play video games as a channel to release their anger and 62 percent of them use video games as a means for relaxation. Also, if video games are such an abomination, you always have the option of monitoring your kids to ensure they are not playing those games. Here's another groundbreaking idea: perhaps you should not buy them those games for Christmas and subject yourself to high interest rates as a result of maxing out your credit cards spending money

you don't have. There is not a single video game that advocates violence. Maybe parents should heed the ESRB ratings and stop looking at a scapegoat when the real culprit's image is the reflection on the mirror.

47. ***You enter your daughters (and sons and transvestites) into beauty contests*** as early as three years of age with the expectation they will not metamorphose into entitled, judgmental, spoiled divas when entering grade school. Yet you fail to understand it is this mentality that breeds bullies who pick on less fortunate kids who do lack the means to buy chic designer clothing, trainers to keep this as thin as a toothpick, perfectly tanned skin, or even ornate hairstyles. No child is born a bully: this is simply a mentality that is bequeathed from parents to children. American parents emphasize perfection in the most superficial and reified of realms such as "beauty" instead of fostering the more commendable approach inculcating that all people are beautiful in their own way. Thank God for companies like Dove who cut through these bullshit parameters beleaguering a rather reified concept of "beauty." It's quite clear this country has yet to learn anything from the unsolved murder of child porn star JonBenet Ramsey and the toxic effects of child beauty pageants.

48. ***You ridicule foreigners because of their "accents,"*** but you fail to understand that you also have an accent yourself whether it is Southern, Northern, Western, Northeastern, Texan, or even Louisianan (since nobody understands those fuckers). The bottom line is everyone has an "accent" that may not be ecumenically intelligible. Whenever I visit India, people laugh at my Hindi citing my accent and saying that it still seems like I am speaking English when I speak Hindi. When you migrate from your native area, your accent will become exotic and you will be the one distraught about the upbraiding the natives hurl at your accent. The only difference is they will not act superior to you since Americans view themselves as superior to any foreigner with an "accent." Then Americans berate those people for not speaking English proficiently. The ironic part

about this situation is the fact those foreigners are investing assiduous effort to learn English as their second and sometimes third language. How many Americans actually place any effort in learning a second language? According to the Department of Education, only 18 percent of Americans report speaking a language other than English at home compared to 53 percent of Europeans. Keep in mind this 18 percent includes the profusion of people that have migrated from all over the world that spoke the foreign language before coming to America. I can bet you that any of those Chinese students who visit America can speak English one thousand times more proficiently than the average American can speak Chinese. Perhaps you should commend the foreigner with an accent for their travail in attempting to learn the English language rather than maligning them for not speaking with the fluency you do being born into it. Of course, Americans will vaingloriously contend they do not need to learn a foreign language because English is a "lingua franca" spoken across the globe. Perhaps Americans should practice some humility since the reason why they can travel anywhere in the world and be accommodated is due to the efforts of the British in how they expanded their empire through Asia, Africa, and even the Pacific Islands. America holds a scanty at best contribution in English becoming a lingua franca. Yet Americans mock the British too for their "accents."

49. ***You use the term "LMAO"*** to emphasize the hilarity of something as if it is physically possible to laugh out of your ass. Then again, this term is fitting for Americans since most of them think out of their asses, ergo; it is not a stretch to conclude they must laugh out of their asses as well. Now it makes sense why the prevailing symbol for the Democratic Party is a donkey and 47 percent of Americans are Democrats according to the Gallup Poll statistics.

50. ***You think a "reality" show is actually real.*** News flash America: reality shows are as scripted as wrestling which we all established as "fake" a long time ago in terms of being scripted. The only difference lies in that wrestling actually requires

remarkable physical skill while being on a "reality" show requires no discernible skill at all aside from being shameless in your willingness to publicize the most intimate details of your life coupled with artificially pumping in drama as ordered by your ventriloquist producer. To underscore my point in case you do not want to take my word for it, I will provide some excerpts directly from the mouth of the svelte "Laguna Beach" and "Hills" alumnus Kristin Cavallari when appearing on "Bethenny." Aside from the disturbing fact that a putz like Bethenny Frankel has her own television show, I'm sure it was equally revolting to hear Cavallari spill the beans about how she "faked relationships and faked fights." To illustrate an example of a "fake relationship," she cited the putative rekindling of an old flame with Brody Jenner. According to Kristin Cavallari in the "eye-opening" interview, Brody Jenner was depicted as dating Jayde Nicole and she added that "They pretended that him and Jayde broke up and I was dating Brody, and Jayde and I got into a huge fight because she saw us in a club. It wasn't real at all. They were together the entire time." Furthermore, she mentioned the fact that her and Brody never dated following their initial breakup despite the show wanting people to believe they started dating again. Cavillari's initial breakup with Brody transpired when she was all of eighteen-years-old after which the nature of her love interest graduated and evolved into pursuing the overrated and underachieving QB type who quits on his team during the middle of an NFC title game only to be spotted partying in a club later that night. The only fools are the American public who ingenuously patronize and subsidize the lavish lifestyle of these maladroit quacks with no acting or professional credentials while there are several thousands of unemployed people with actual credentials and degrees struggling to pay rent with the ponderous education loan debts looming. Keep watching these sordid shows about worthless buffoons partying on your dime as if it will coruscate the wretched reality construing your life.

51. *You think this movement to "political correctness" is salutary* when in fact it is a form of totalitarianism. When

you look at all forms of totalitarianism throughout history, they all share a common thread delineated by conformity to a certain belief or mindset. In the case of "political correctness," we are all forced to conform to a certain mindset abrogating the use of any kind of language deemed "offensive" and "inappropriate." Anyone who unwittingly or precipitously utilizes such language regardless of the context is subject to personal and professional ostracism which I regard as a form of persecution. Essentially, just like the Nazis, Communists, Baathists, or any other totalitarian based regime through world history, people with dissenting ideas or beliefs are essentially being singled out as pariahs and undesirables. Anyone who is a homophobe is subject to getting fired, disbanded, or dissociated from an organization. Thus, you are essentially persecuting people who are trying to practice their religions—many of which advocate that homosexuality is sinful. Thus, under the guise of "political correctness," society is itself curtailing basic first amendment rights such as freedom of speech and freedom of religion. John Stuart Mill once said the three dangers of democracy are bureaucracies, demagogues, and conformity. The fires of "political correctness" have fanned and permeated across the landscape of America on the strength of all three mediums mentioned by John Stuart Mill. Now it is threatening the livelihood of the basic freedoms Americans implicitly took for granted under the US Constitution. You have bureaucrats in their ivory towers enacting counterproductive "anti-discrimination" and "sexual harassment" clauses in work contracts to the extent they are stunting the career development of several talented people whose personal beliefs are not "politically correct." As for the demagogues, they protrude in the form of the bleeding hearts present in the media who ruthlessly attack violators of the "political correctness" doctrine like bloodsucking vampires. Look at how they destroyed the livelihood of an extremely talented celebrity cook Paula Deen because she admitted to using racial slurs toward her subordinates in the past. It is as if those racial slurs completely nullify the fact that she is an extremely gifted cook who shared many spectacular recipes with millions of people in her top selling cookbooks over the years. Not to mention her sexual harassment and discrimination suit were both dropped quite possibly due to a lack of merit. It is stupefying to me that someone could become a social pariah without committing an actual prosecutable offense. Her crime entails exercising her first amendment rights to express views of a race that many people probably hold, but lack the jewels to promulgate it due to the threat of ostracism concomitant with violating the unwritten "Political Correctness Act." The "Political Correctness Act" makes the Patriot Act seem as commendable as the Civil Rights Act of 1965. At least the Patriot Act attempts to target speech serving as a threat to national security while the speech probed by the Political Correctness Act really does not threaten the life of any person. Sorry folks: calling a black man a "nigga" or "nigger" does not really constitute a material threat to their lives. It may hurt their fragile feelings, but they will get over it once they chomp down on a twelve-piece bucket of fried chicken wings, collard greens, and mashed potatoes to go along with their raspberry flavored Kool-Aid. If you call a Jewish person a "kike," they might turn lachrymose until they reach home, open up their bank statement, realize they are still fluid, and then remind themselves of the fact that Jews own America. If you call a Hispanic person a "spic," they might turn as acrid as an avocado before going back home and eating a few slices of avocados to go along with their burritos, enchiladas, tacos, tamales, and nachos they eat every night. Then they will wake up to the reality of being the fastest growing demographic in America. Man does it suck for those xenophobic Republicans now that Hispanics are voting in droves. If you call a Chinese woman "lady chinky eyes"(like a Papa John's worker unwittingly did on a receipt back in 2011), she might harangue for a few free pizzas before going back home to drench herself in fried rice and Kung Pao chicken. Then she will wake up to the fact Mandarin is the most spoken language in the world and China has the United States by the balls economically speaking. Not to mention Chinese immigrants are kicking American ass in the classroom. Hence the unofficial meaning of UCLA being University of Caucasians Losing to Asians. My point is every race/ethnicity/culture is uniquely spectacular and they all contribute to making America sui generis in terms of cultural diversity. The stereotypes I mentioned earlier in jest may have been offensive, but they are meaningless unless we persistently try to quash them under the guise of "political correctness." Anytime you try to censor "hate speech" in the form of racial slurs and stereotypes, you only serve to give them greater credibility. Maybe it's time to just ignore the incendiary speech of racist people and just focus on whatever personal goals you want to achieve in life. Once you ignore racists long enough, they will realize their behavior is otiose and they might cease using racially charged language. It's like when a child is throwing a tantrum; a psychologist will tell you the best thing to do would be to ignore the child until they cease the puerile behavior. The child will acknowledge this hostile behavior is ineffectual and they will start behaving calmly to get your attention. When the parent actively reacts to a tantrum throwing child, they are essentially giving the power to the child and sending the message that all it takes is a tantrum from them to garner the parent's attention. A racist is just like a child deep inside. When you stop giving attention to their philippic race rants, they will eventually cease the undesirable behavior voluntarily. Then everyone walks home happy without feeling oppressed; however, in the au courant atmosphere of "political correctness," many people are getting oppressed, repressed, and socially ostracized just for expressing dissent which evinces a fundamental first amendment right.

52. ***You find it acceptable to celebrate "Black History Month" in the shortest month of the year*** (February). Forget the fact you are demeaning and trivializing the African-American experience by only devoting one month of the year to it. Forget the fact that month falls on average the shortest month in the calendar. The most disturbing fact is the propensity of American society to sequester "Black history" from regular American history. The bottom line is "Black history" is indeed American history from the time they were brought onto ships from Africa, subjected to chattel slavery, built underground

railroads to escape slavery in the South, fought in the Civil War, and their travail during the Civil Rights Movement culminating in the freedoms that most of us take for granted today. I find it reprehensible that under the guise of "political correctness" we feel it is appropriate to even utilize the term "Black history" when American history would not be relevant without the contribution of African Americans. Think about any of the major monuments in this country, particularly in cities like DC, Philadelphia, Boston, and New York. All of them were essentially built with some profound form of African American labor. It is the struggle of African Americans through the centuries which essentially made America a paragon for cultural diversity, racial harmony, and human dignity. America did not embody any of those principles when the white settlers ravaged the Natives or when the white settlers enslaved blacks to work on their plantations. America did not embody these principles when the Founding Fathers penned a Constitution that did not even view the blacks as actual people. America did not embody those principles when they were mired in a tumultuous Civil War. If you want to know what makes America great, look at the evolution of the African American through the course of American history. If their struggle does not fully embody the genuine trials, tribulations, and triumph of America, then I'm not sure what will suffice. Sure, the white people have made an indispensable contribution to American prosperity, but it is the struggle of the African Americans which have taken America to an unprecedented level of social prosperity evincing the envy of the world. Thus, we should incorporate "Black history" as a natural facet of the disquisition on American history without any sequestration. At the end of the day, America is a land of immigrants and it's time we celebrated all of our immigrants' contributions concurrently.

Update: I want to take this opportunity to excoriate the media and the incredulous American public for their irresponsible handling of the whole Donald Sterling saga. For those of you who do not follow NBA basketball, he was the owner of the Los Angeles Clippers who received a Draconian sentence from NBA

Commissioner Adam Silver banning him from attending any NBA games with a concomitant $2.5 million fine. This sentence came as a denouement stemming from Sterling's sullen and seemingly invidious remarks pertaining to African Americans in a private conversation with his model girlfriend. While I concur his comments were saturnine and reprehensible, he does have a right to privacy and freedom of speech just like every other American. Even if he is a "racist slumlord," the first amendment still protects him the same way it protects "humanitarian" Bill Gates. I am more appalled by the fact nobody expressed indignation over the fact this man's right to privacy got trampled upon by an overzealous TMZ reporter with assistance from Sterling's ironically mixed race girlfriend. The bottom line is you could record anyone's private conversations and be subject to hearing inappropriate, racist, sexist, and inflammatory remarks. Hence that construes why we call them "private" since we expect privacy. Of course, this expectation of privacy entails naivety since someone is always listening to every "secure" conversation to ensure nobody is plotting a "jihad" or an "intifada" or even planning to institute "Sharia" law in America. Clearly there is no compelling public interest to allow Sterling's "lover's quarrel" conversations broadcasted for the entire world to hear. His conversations are not a matter of national security and he deserves some measure of protection in terms of his private conversations. The most egregious aspect of this ordeal is the fact he is being castigated and socially crucified just for expressing an unpopular (a.k.a. "politically incorrect") viewpoint. Essentially, the NBA penalized him $2.5 million for comments made in a private conversation having little bearing on the NBA nor did it entail utilizing NBA resources to promulgate those remarks. I believe the NBA presumptuously invoked their powers to fine and sanction an individual just because of unpopular beliefs. It is as though the first amendment has been relegated to relic status in the contemporary world as it only applies to "politically correct" speech. In this case, let's just abrogate the first amendment altogether since we all seem content to curtail it under the specious guise of "political correctness." Even though most Americans seem content on ignoring history, the fact of the matter is the first amendment was penned by our Founding Fathers to protect unpopular speech. Furthermore, it was formulated to deter a forced "groupthink" amongst a populace in order to enable a free-flowing exchange of ideas to ultimately fuel a healthy democracy. Now society is adamant on extirpating first amendment protections on "unpopular" speech in favor of levying opprobrium, ostracism, and suspicion on anyone that is not pro-Semite, homophilic, Afro-philic, and nihilistic. Now it seems we are promoting the same conformity in thinking that the framers of our Constitution fought assiduously against when spearheading the Bill of Rights. The media successfully brainwashed the fatuous American public into believing Donald Sterling's demise evinced a day of triumph when in fact it signified another setback for the meaningful exercise of the first amendment. For me, it represented a day of despair because Americans are too infatuated and blinded by the gilded nature of "political correctness" to realize their basic liberties lie in a perilous condition. They feel to realize the first amendment is under attack and nobody seems to give a damn anymore because we all strive for the "political correctness" that shunts the mellifluous flow of thoughts and ideas imperative to a functional democracy. Even if Sterling's comments are repugnant, we as a society cannot rejoice when institutions take it upon themselves to enforce punitive measures for "unpopular speech." Instead, we as a society must become clever by using our powers of boycotting and protest to force Sterling's hand. That will hit him in a place where he would feel it most as a businessman: the wallet. However, punishing someone for the mere exercise of free speech perilously places society on a slippery slope leading down the alley of totalitarianism. Maybe that's what Americans ultimately crave: a totalitarian government that tells us how to think, eat, drink, breathe, and live. Otherwise, it would behoove society to stop thinking, eating, drinking, breathing, and living the societal poison of "political correctness."

53. ***You harass and levy suspicion upon people who are praying in public.*** I will have to admit this one strikes a personal chord. In Boston, I dealt with this treatment on several occasions.

Two instances come to mind. The first one was while I was performing one of my daily prayers on the first floor of the medical school building before one of my classes. After my prayer was done, a security officer approached me and asserted they were receiving complaints about my "suspicious" behavior. Thus, some parochial minded dimwit piqued because I exercised my first amendment rights contrary to their understanding of the Constitution which can be summed up by the belief of "freedom from religion" rather than "freedom of religion." The second instance emanated a few months later a few hundred yards from Fenway Park when I awaited the arrival of my friends. It also coincided with the time for my early evening prayer which I performed on the sidewalk of one of the relatively quiet crossroads leading to Fenway. After I finished the prayer, a police officer on his motorcycle approached me and immediately understood I was praying. He then proceeded to tell me that he received complaints from certain people who thought I was engaging in "suspicious and potentially psychotic" behavior. Then he exclaimed "I apologize for the inconvenience caused by some ignorant people who fail to understand you are praying." This police officer happened to be one of the few classy and cognizant people I met in Boston. Before I lived in Boston, I held the perception it was one of the more culturally sophisticated cities in the world. After living there for nearly three years, it became quite clear that most people in that city are provincial minded, pretentious buffoons that have probably never prayed in their life and get a rise out of harassing people that actually believe in God. Keep in mind I attended Florida State University and I generally prayed outside the main Strozier Library where hundreds of people could observe me. Not once was I ever approached by a security officer at Florida State (or Tallahassee at large) concerning complaints of "suspicious behavior" from other people pertaining to my prayer. Supposedly Tallahassee has the reputation of being in the heart of "redneck country" while Boston is arrogated as a culturally resplendent gem. My experiences indicate an antithesis of both perceptions. Not to mention the fact many Boston residents abortively protested the development of the ISBCC mosque on Malcolm X Boulevard as if the first amendment right to freedom of religion does not apply to Muslims anymore. Apparently the Yahudi sycophants at the Boston Globe arrogated the idea the project received funding from an organization involved in "terrorist" activity. Then again, if we used the warped American definition encompassing "terrorist" activity, any practice of Islam falls under that penumbra. Until the constitutional law catches up with the American definition of terrorism, it appears that we Muslims still have the right to practice our bellicose, misogynist, savage, and xenophobic religion. On the flip side, nobody ever protested the development of the mosques in Tallahassee. Perhaps there is more religious tolerance down South than up North possibly because people down South are not anorexic to all forms of religious practice as they are up North in morally bereft areas like Boston and NYC.

54. ***You argue over whether the best pizza comes from New York City (flat, foldable style), Chicago (deep dish) or New Haven (brick oven)*** when in fact the best pizza comes from the place of pizza's origin in Naples, Italy. In fact, the NYC style pizza is a slight variation of the pizza hailing from Naples. That would be as asinine as Boston, Detroit, and Pittsburgh fans arguing over who is the best hockey town when everyone knows Montreal is the greatest hockey town in the world with the most passionate fans. Not to mention the fact that modern ice hockey was invented in Montreal by a student from the esteemed McGill University. When are Americans going to realize that you cannot ever top the original? Then again, if Americans ever came up with anything originally instead of stealing everyone else's ideas, they may understand. Sorry folks: macaroni and cheese is just a bastardized version of the elbow pasta which came from Italia.

55. ***You wear sunglasses as large as the Big Ben clock in London*** when your eyes are the size of a nail. Sorry, but I have to confess I stole this gripe from the vivacious Cat Valentine character played by the multi-talented entertainment maven

Ariana Grande in both "Victorious" and "Sam and Cat." As Cat Valentine exclaimed "Why do you need such big glasses? Your eyes are not even that big!"

56. ***You gloat over the fact a Canadian team has not won the Stanley Cup in over twenty years.*** However, you fail to take into account that only seven of the thirty teams in the NHL are from Canada. If we do the math correctly, this means there is a 76.7 percent chance for an American team to win the Stanley Cup every season. Thus, the Stanley Cup is 3.3 times more likely to stay in America every year. We are not exactly comparing apples to apples here. Not to mention the fact most of the players on the elite American teams are from Canada. Of all the players in the NHL, 53.1 percent of them are Canadians. As for the most recent Stanley Cup champions (Chicago Blackhawks), 55 percent of their roster consisted of Canadians. On the 2012 Stanley Cup championship squad of the Los Angeles Kings, a staggering 68 percent of the roster hailed from Canada. Even a majority of the stalwart Boston and Pittsburgh squads are from Canada including arguably the best hockey player in the world (when healthy) in Sidney Crosby. I know it is an American habit to bite the hand that feeds them, but it is preposterous to mock Canadian hockey when all the elite NHL squads are packed with Canadians. It's just a travesty Canadian teams cannot seem to garner enough of that blue chip native talent to win the Cup. However, they have no problem kicking American ass in the Winter Olympics as Canada hoisted the hockey gold medal in three of the last four Winter Olympics while the United States was busy getting emasculated by a country (Finland) that is 1/29th its size for the bronze medal. Yeah, America is so amazing at hockey!

57. ***You precipitously jumped on the media bandwagon while socially crucifying Mike Rice***—the former Rutgers men's head basketball coach. Yeah, there were some videos of him verbally abusing his players and throwing basketballs at them. Yet you failed to acknowledge the fact those videos were released by a vindictive, disgruntled former employee who illegally possessed

them since they were property of Rutgers University. Thus, when Rutgers released him from employment, it was incumbent upon him to return the tapes constituting property of Rutgers University. Instead, he utilized those tapes as blackmail when his extortion attempt sailed south. This whole ordeal provides a microcosmic view of everything awry with American society as coaches are no longer allowed to discipline or hold their players accountable for mistakes. Mike Rice inherited a downtrodden Rutgers program who failed to qualify for the NCAA tournament for two decades before he arrived in 2011. Furthermore, this is a program, which has not won a tournament game since 1983. Rutgers knew what they were getting from Mike Rice when they hired him: a rugged minded disciplinarian driven to whip his players into shape. Mike Rice possessed a strong track record for success as he led Robert Morris to three Northeastern Conference league championships and back to back NCAA tournament appearances in 2009 and 2010. Keep in mind Robert Morris had not made it to the NCAA tournament in the fifteen years prior to his arrival. Clearly Mike Rice proved himself as a winner and tried to shape Rutgers into a winner through discipline and rigorous attention to detail. Yes, some of his language and tactics would be considered abrasive, but these are part of the same attributes that made him a winner at Robert Morris. I am sure if someone taped a practice of luminary coaches like Mike Krzyzewski (a.k.a. Coach K), Rick Pitino, Bill Self, Tom Izzo, and Tom Crean, you would probably observe a few curse words, salty language, and possibly some taps on the chest of players to motivate them. Where was the outrage at the physical contact Phil Jackson hurled at Pau Gasol during game 3 of the Western Conference Semifinals in 2011 against the Mavs when he was seen slapping Pau Gasol on the chest? That could be construed as violent physical contact as well by the tepid standards of the American media. What about Coach K in the 1998 Elite 8 game against UK when he grabbed Rashad McLeod by the jersey near his throat and jerked him forward? There was no media outcry at that point. However, the media chose to attack Mike Rice because he is not a "legendary" coach like

Phil Jackson and Coach K. Furthermore, he evinced an easy target for them to advance their sordid agenda as his Rutgers teams were struggling finishing near the bottom of the Big East conference in his three seasons there. Moreover, if Mike Rice was such a diabolical and cantankerous individual like the incredulous American media wanted everyone to believe, why did many of his former players at the Rutgers come to his defense after his firing? Two players in particular (Wally Judge and Austin Johnson) used adjectives like "big brother," "player's coach," and "someone who did a great deal for them socially and academically" to describe their former coach. Even a former player (Sean Bannon) mentioned how he never felt uncomfortable or threatened when working with Rice and most of the players echoed his sentiment. All the players admitted the tapes provided an extremely narrow lens in its view of Rice's practices and did not fully represent how Rice typically interacted with his players. The testimony of these athletes suggests Mike Rice was actually an upstanding man who inculcated concrete values and principles to them on a workaday basis on and off the court. As far as I am concerned, the media's view of Mike Rice is as judicious as if someone compiled a list of Lebron James' 10–20 worst moments of his basketball career and used it as sole evidence to argue Lebron James is the most overrated basketball player in NBA history on the basis of those 10–20 plays. Heck, you can take any human being under a microscope and pick out an assorted selection of their worst moments to make them look nefarious. The American media has made a habit of cherry picking certain instances, taking them out of context, and distorting facts to destroy reputations in order to advance their insidious agenda. In this instance, they did it riding the back of a vindictive parasite lacking credibility to begin with. They clearly followed this cognate pattern in pulverizing Mike Rice's career. Let's give ESPN and the other corporate American media parasites a pat on the back.

58. *You wear a "cocktail" dress in public* in which you expose your back, your legs from the thigh downward, and your ass. Yet you act as though you do not want a "cock" to go through

your "tail" later on that night even though that's probably one of the main reasons you decided to dress like a glorified hooker.

59. ***You use tanning beds*** in lieu of the beach to avoid the harmful sun exposure. However, tanning beds expose your skin to pernicious UV-A and UV-B rays both of which damage skin and contribute to eventual cancer. In addition, the buffoon women who use tanning beds expose themselves to a 75 percent greater risk of contracting melanoma. I am sure exposing your skin to impending skin cancer is worth becoming golden brown like the fries and tater tots you munch on while you are not dallying at the tanning salon. Anytime I see a woman with a tan, I feel like pouring mustard, onions, and chives on top of her and commencing my breakfast. Another fun fact: nearly 30 percent of white female high school students use tanning beds. The up and coming trend within the next few years will be African American, Asian, and Hispanic women bleaching their skin so they can act and feel as dumb as most white women. Then again, learning to become as fatuous as a white woman evinces as rigorous of a discipline as a four-year petroleum engineering major.

60. ***You walk on the street with flip flops, a large t-shirt (even though your frame is as diminutive as an Oompa-Loompa) and very short skirts*** that essentially pass as glorified panties. The only problem is that someone would need to pull your shirt up to confirm that you are actually wearing something below your waist. This is a trend on college campuses as well as concentrated shopping centers. I guess it's a woman's subtle signal of being "hot and ready" like a pizza from Little Caesar's for an encounter since they already did you a favor by taking off their own pants. Maybe it's their answer to the ghetto blacks with their pants hanging down below their asses perhaps priming themselves for a "hot and ready" encounter of their own. Just like the Little Caesar's "hot and ready" pizzas, they are crass and tasteless.

61. ***You use the term "African American"*** because someone's ancestors were forced to migrate from Africa on ships about four centuries ago. Why aren't white people designated as

"European Americans" since the ancestors of all the "garden variety" whites emanated from European countries? Anyone with a sliver of intelligence realizes the current "African Americans" are as sequestered, disillusioned, and detached from African culture as Miley Cyrus is to being a traditional Southern girl with Christian values (as she frequently purported before the Vanity Fair shoot in 2008). It's time for Americans to charter some consistency in their racial designations. Either we use the terms "black" and "white" in conjunction if we want to emphasized perceived relative appearance or we use "African American" and "European American" together if we want to emphasize ancestral origin. This convenient mixing and matching obfuscates the actual anthropological, historical, and social context accompanying the concept of race in this country. As a précis, stop designating blacks as "African Americans" because they are not African just like pyrite is not gold. Pyrite may share certain superficial characteristics with gold, but it is not sold as gold aside from a few stores owned by conniving mountebanks.

62.   ***You feel underage drinking is acceptable.*** I know math is not a forte amongst Americans, but the legal age for drinking across the United States is twenty-one. Most college-going individuals matriculate at the age of eighteen, which is less than twenty-one last time I checked. Thus, it should be illegal for most college kids as well. However, you would not know that if you checked out Florida State University's (my alma mater) self-reported statistics on their own students. In a 2012 CORE Survey, FSU boasted about the fact that a staggering 20 percent of their students reported they do not drink. Theoretically, that means upwards of 80 percent of the student population is breaking the law by consuming alcohol illegally. Yay, only 80 percent of our students are breaking the law! We are a model institution! Of course, most of you will contend that college students are a chronologically diverse group and there are not necessarily 75 percent of college students who are below twenty-one years of age. However, according to a study from the Century Council (a neat non-profit organization funded

by alcohol distillers), 82 percent of college students under the age of twenty-one admitted to alcohol consumption. That debunks any argument that most college going kids that drink are older than twenty-one. Moreover, the problem is just as egregious amongst middle and high school aged children. The 2011 Monitoring the Future Survey asserted 33 percent of eighth graders and 70 percent of twelfth graders admitted to the consumption of alcohol. Furthermore, the Office of Juvenile Justice and Delinquency Prevention reported that individuals aged twelve to twenty years accounted for 11 percent of all alcohol consumption in the United States. Yet most of these high school and university white-collar administrative buffoons in the outlandish and vacuous assembly speeches choose to emphasize "safe drinking" and "designated driver" rhetoric instead of promulgating that alcohol is an illicit, certified poison for that age group. Essentially, that is white collar speak for waving the white flag on curbing the act of underage drinking in favor of simply curbing the residual effects of underage drinking stemming from drunk driving. Yet they ignore the pernicious effects of alcohol on the individual level manifesting in social, mental, and physical problems. You would think high schools would be more serious about combating alcohol use considering all the potential funding they lose due to lagging attendance stemming from alcohol related hangovers. Keep on telling (and failing) these kids by telling them alcohol consumption is okay as long as you have a designated driver and drink a phantom "safe" amount.

63. ***You pronounce Pakistan as though you just got finished playing a classic video game*** where a yellow specimen eats dots and travels through a maze while avoiding assorted colored monsters. Or maybe you are just thinking of the twelve or twenty-four packs you are going to buy tonight for the blocKeg party you are going to throw this weekend. Chances are the gas station you utilize to buy the alcohol is owned by a Pack-i-stani. Okay, not really since 50 percent of the gas stations in America are owned by Indians instead of the hapless Pakistanis. However, there are many Pakistani gas station owners included

in the mighty Asian American Convenience Store Association (AACSA), which convenes in an annual conference to exchange tactics on how to screw over their vendors by using their large refrigerators without buying much of their actual product. They also discuss how to screw over their employees and the government alike by working their employees like indentured slaves without paying them overtime or giving them a W2. Thus, they do not have to report their employees' income to the government. As an Indian myself, I do not harbor any resentment for the invectives most Americans hurl at Indian/Pakistani (which I will term as "Desi") gas station owners because most of them are insidious scumbags of the highest order. These Desi owners make the Sopranos appear as virtuous as the Brady Bunch and they deserve all invidious acts levied their way. The worst amongst them are the equivocal Pakistani gas station owners who claim to be Muslim yet sell and vigorously profit off religiously abrogated items such as alcohol, cigarettes, and pork-based products. This is tantamount to a Quaker owning a gun shop profiting off violent weapons despite the Quaker denunciation of any and all forms of violence. So let me say it: you are *not* a TAA if you hate Desi gas station owners because even regular Desi detest them.

By the way, it just hit me: if you combine Pakistan and Turkmenistan, you get Pakmenistan where you have little yellow creatures with absent-slice mouths and sunken eyes that consume all the meat, oil, coal, greenery, pork, and luxury goods in its path. Oh wait a minute; the Chinese already possess the copyright to that description (of voracious yellow creatures) and accompanying role in the world market). Perhaps the purpose of creating the Pacman game in the first place was to portentously foreshadow China's desire to eventually consume the entire world one television set at a time.

64. *You spend thousands of dollars a year on cable, internet, or satellite pornography* when you could just go on YouTube and view it for free. As of the time and date (10/1/2013 11:48 PM CST) I put in a search for pornography on YouTube, there

were 3,590,000 different videos for pornography. I am sure a myriad of them are teasers, but even if 20 percent are legit, that means there are over 700,000 real pornographic videos for free on YouTube. Yet, Americans spend $12 billion a year on pornography according to Brigham Young University's Women's Services Department. They also expanded on this statistic claiming it exceeds the collective revenue of the NBA, NFL, and MLB. According to a November 2011 edition of Addiction Treatment magazine, upwards of 25 percent of Americans are viewing pornographic material at work leading to profound productivity losses from Sea to Shining See Nude People. The most ironic part of the BYU study entails two other factoids about pornography in the United States obtained from the Online Schools organization. First, Utah has the highest porn subscription rate in the country amongst broadband internet users at 5.47 per user. I guess it mirrors their supremacy in wives per man. Then again, one can understand why Utah possesses the highest rate since they lack an NFL, NHL, and MLB professional team. Not to mention their lone professional team Utah Jazz' demise since Jerry Sloan's retirement has them mired in free fall mode. As for the Utah Utes, life has been rough in the Pac 12 while BYU is still adjusting to their independence in terms of scheduling enough quality teams to make them a legitimate national title contender one day instead of miring in a middle-tier bowl after their nine win season. The most pressing factor is the lack of strip clubs or anything remotely entertaining nightlife-wise across Mormon Land. Thus, the home computer is the only outlet to a real nightlife for a Utah man or woman since the seven wives are not doing a good enough job of satisfying the Mormon man. The second factoid resonating from the Online Schools report concerns Sunday being the most popular day of the week to indulge in pornographic viewing. It tells you how superannuated the church service has become in the American landscape when only 17.7 percent of Christians attend the Sunday service while a sizeable chunk of the rest are potentially and seemingly doing the opposite of church. If you want a source for that 17.7 percent figure, it comes from an actual director of church planning for the Evangelical Church. This same figure was more or less corroborated by sociologists C. Kirk Hadaway and Penny Long Marler in a 2005 article published in *The Journal for the Scientific Study of Religion*. For the longest time, these church dodging Christians would cite reasons such as football (which only holds weight for like five months in a year) for missing the service. The problem with that excuse entails the fact NFL football games generally start in the afternoon at 1 PM EST and 12 PM CST or even late morning in the Mountain Time region. On the other hand, church services are generally offered in the morning starting at 8:00 and last about two to two and a half hours. Unless you are attending the actual game or tailgating at the actual event, I doubt you need more than an hour to preen yourself to watch a football game after that arduous church service. Now it's become quite clear what many of them might be doing before and after their real Sunday ritual of watching football. I guess there is not much of a debate between attending a sententious sermon and getting your morning porn fix. So what if you are committing fornication with your eyes? If you're a Catholic, all you have to do is confess to your father, drink some holy water and you will be forgiven. It would not hurt if you contributed "a little sumtin sumtin" to the settlement fund for the inevitable child molestation cases stemming from the licentious activities of your pedophile priests and bishops.

65. ***You post "selfies" of yourself doing mundane activities*** like brushing your teeth, brushing your hair, applying your makeup (revealing why you need makeup in the first place a la Sarah Jessica Parker), and popping your pimples (a.k.a. breakouts). Meanwhile you are dressed in your scanty prebed or postwake up attire as if you are preparing for a Victoria's Secret shoot. Of course, it is slightly more revealing than the bedizen attire you perfunctorily wear in public anyway thus diffusing the level of shame associated with your glorified lingerie shoot. Perhaps you should think about the fact your profile is publicly available to the extent your parents could view those asinine "selfies." Essentially, you are publicizing details of your personal life that

your parents do not want to become privy of let alone everyone in the world. Pretty soon, people will take selfies of them urinating, expectorating, or vomiting following a hangover.

66. ***You issue death threats to celebrities*** who may express even the slightest hint of interest in dating your favorite celebrity. I felt some sympathy for Kim Kardashian after being assailed with death threats following the mere promulgation that she would hook up with Justin Bieber—a sentiment mimicked by 99.9 percent of American women at the time when he was just an innocent albeit good looking boy (which seems like ages ago). For all her crucifiable (not really a word, but bear with me) activities, you choose to target her for something she purportedly uttered in jest in order to satiate your delusional fantasy of being Bieber's primary make-believe love interest. Keep in mind this is the same woman who spearheaded a specious Philippines typhoon victim fundraiser on eBay only to retain 90 percent of the funds for herself. Moreover, there is a 99.999999999999 percent chance you will never meet Justin Bieber in an intimate setting and an even higher chance he will not even give you the time of day. Even if she was hypothetically interested in Justin Bieber, what right does anyone have to infringe upon her quest for the Biebs (my apologies to Jeanette McCurdy for vitiating that term)? How outraged would you act if other people within or even outside your friend circle sent you death threats for pursuing a relationship with someone else who is single and available? That brings me to my second point about the supposed death threats the comely belle Ariana Grande received from the obtuse Nathan Sykes votaries as a result of pursuing a potential relationship with him. These death threats occluded the two from admitting their courtship earlier until it became painfully obvious when they were spotted latching onto each other like Siamese twins at Disney World as if they super glued their hands. It's amazing how obtuse many American Twitteradicals are to the extent they would be willing to risk jail time and inflict terror on another person to display their devotion to someone that's not even cognizant of their existence. I know

many of these celebrities claim to love their fans, but it's quite obvious to those of us with brains these celebrities lack the bandwidth to become familiar with even 0.001 percent of their fans. Maybe you should invest that energy in something that will directly benefit you like obtaining an education or social and technical skills that will allow you to get a job instead of freeloading off your parents and/or the government. Of course, daydreaming about Justin Bieber from the comfort of your parent's basement convincing yourself of the subliminal messages he is sending you also works.

67. ***You put your face (and other undisclosed locations of your body) through plastic surgery.*** I know people will view me as sententious, but I am unapologetic in my belief in one god (Allah s.b.w.t). I believe God created man and women in upright form and there is no reason for us to change our physical appearance. Since most Americans have relegated to apostate status in relation to believing in God, I will use a "scientific" basis to explain how obtuse plastic surgery is with the exception of the exigent cases involving burning/scarring of skin due to fire. First of all, if you want a poster child for everything wrong with plastic surgery, look at Heidi Montag (or Pratt). There was a point in time when this congenial small town Colorado girl was actually comely and had a bright future ahead of her. Now she looks like a love child between Slimer from Ghostbusters and the Michelin Man from the tire commercials. In short, she looks like mayonnaise on an ash tray. If seeing how hideous she has become does not dissuade you from pursuing plastic surgery, maybe the physical health aspect of it can do the trick. Plastic surgery has been linked to excessive blood clotting and aggregation underneath the skin referred to as hematoma. Sure, it generally goes away within a day, but there is a chance this hematoma could exacerbate which manifests in decreased oxygen glow to the blood resulting in skin death. Furthermore, it can lead to "scarring" of skin tissue, necrosis (fancy scientific argot meaning death of tissues due to lack of oxygen which gets catalyzed by smoking), and nerve damage (in the form of paralysis of

muscles). All these adverse side effects are accompanied by more surgery which serves to deplete your bank account with profound celerity. Oh yeah, I forgot to mention it figuratively (and sometimes literally) costs you an arm and a leg. Not to mention the potential for adverse reactions to anesthesia which most of the sleazebag plastic surgeons will gloss over anyway when performing your consultation. Most of all, you are exposing yourself to the pleasant garden-variety nosocomial infections present in any hospital setting. As you could probably surmise from the name itself, these cannot be palliated as your proverbial "speed bumps" since they include fever, inflammation in the area of the procedure, and discharge of viscous yellowish or white fluid. Keep in mind 5–10 percent of all patients receive nosocomial infections from hospitals according to the Gale Encyclopedia of Public Health. Of course, people will argue these are a) minor complications and b) rare occurrences. Let's assume both are true for a New York minute. Is it worth blowing a crater sized hole through your bank account and exposing yourself to extraneous risks surrounding hospital infections, adverse symptoms stemming from anesthetics and the surgery itself just so you can feel a little more beautiful? Now onto the psychological implications of this decision, perhaps you should consider how it can adversely affect your relationship with the people that matter the most in your life (or should matter the most) such as your parents, siblings, friends, and significant others. If any of them are advocating for you to obtain plastic surgery, perhaps you should cut off that cord because these are the people that genuinely love you for who you are. The bottom line is every human being has physical, mental, and psychological frailties. Appreciation of these limitations and weaknesses is what allows people to obtain success in life rather than trying to eliminate them. As Anne Wallace (an actual chief of plastic surgery at the prestigious UCSD Health System) said, patients are often surprised that altering one area of the body generates complications in another part of the body which further disturbs the homeostasis of the body. She used an example of Botox injections as generating not only plump lips, but an errant nose. Thus, we are brought back to the First Law of Thermodynamics which states energy is neither created or destroyed, but rather it is transformed. Plastic surgery conforms to this law analogously by failing to eliminate the problem, but rather transforming the area of the problem to other potentially less flattering places.

68. ***You feel the need to obtain breast implants*** to increase your "stock" as a woman. First of all, if you are infatuated with the idea of being a movie starlet or some kind of performer in show business, take a look at Kate Hudson before 2010 when she impetuously decided to obtain breast implants. Let's just say her assets were back loaded during that time, but people noticed that her breasts were ostensibly petite. However, that did not prevent her from boasting a superlatively successful movie career including fifteen award-winning performances from accredited film bodies as well as twenty-seven nominations. Most notably, she won an Academy Award for her performance in "Almost Famous." The bottom line is there are several gals in the performance industry that struck success on the basis of their talent rather than superficial characteristics. Enlarging your breasts does not necessarily enhance your talent level nor does it work any wonders for your brain contrary to popular opinion. Moreover, it's actually pretty harmful. According to a University of Michigan Department of Plastic Surgery study, saline breast surgery carries a 27.6 percent risk of complications. According to Dr. Nalini Chilkov (an oriental medical doctor and Founder of IntegrativeCancerAnswers. com), there are twenty-three conspicuous complications of breast surgery. For the sake of brevity and non-redundancy from point no. 67, breast surgery is actually related to arthritis and joint pain, metal poisoning due to exposure of platinum endemic to silicone implants, autoimmune diseases such as fibromyalgia in which nerves are consistently firing, chronic breast pain, limited breastfeeding capacity, and most of all, greater difficulty in identifying risk of breast cancer due to rupturing of the implants stemming from pressure applied by the mammogram itself. You may question Dr. Chilkov's

assessment of the situation since she is a proponent of natural medicine; however, all of her promulgations are corroborated in the report published by the National Research Center for Women and Families. We know this group just wants what's best for women and it's clear that breast implants are far from salutary to the point of being deleterious. When considering any type of surgery or any course of action in general, it is always imperative to weigh the benefits and risks. In this case, the risks are gargantuan, but the benefits are dubious. There is no guarantee larger breasts will make you feel better about yourself. In fact, they may contribute to further ostracism and self-pity all at an exorbitant cost. People may view you as desperate for attention. To me, deciding to obtain breast implants is tantamount to entering a ghost chili pepper eating contest. Even if you win the contest, was it worth burning off your tongue and permanently damaging your taste buds? The perceived pride obtained from procuring a breast implant is not worth that much of a risk nor is it worth the physical, emotional, psychological, and economic burdens accompanying it.

69. ***You find girls kissing other girls amusing.*** Since I am a practicing Muslim, my views on homosexuality should be obvious, thus, I feel no need to further delineate what I feel about homosexuality. In fact, this is not even an indictment of homosexuality. The idea of heterosexual women making out with other heterosexual (or even homosexual) women is disturbing and I feel it directly mocks real homosexual women who genuinely are attracted to women rather than men. It's tantamount to wearing a neck brace when you do not have a neck injury or even walking with a cane or crutch when you are ambulatory. Clearly, it's a patronizing act to make it appear as though you are empathizing with them when you are in reality mocking the perceived bizarre behavior/ condition. According to the Cosmo Poll taken in 2008, 54 percent of females aged eighteen to twenty-four reported locking lips with another female while that number modestly ebbed to 43 percent for women between the ages of twenty-five and thirty-four.

Furthermore, a 2012 study done by Megan Yost and Lauren McCarthy published in the journal named "Psychology of Woman Quarterly" investigated this homosexual activity of otherwise heterosexual females. Amongst their detailed findings, 69 percent of college women and men reported observing two girls making out at a party while 33 percent of women admitted making out with another woman themselves at these parties. While it's unclear how many of these women admired the likes of Brittany Spears, Madonna, Scarlett Johansson, Sandra Bullock, or even Katy Perry (who shamelessly perpetuates the allure of this salacious behavior), it is clear these women are nihilists who are more confused about their own sexuality than they may want to admit. If we as a society are preaching "tolerance" toward homosexuality, does it really make much sense to mimic the behavior just to prove you are "tolerant" toward it? For example, we prove our "tolerance" of many religious faiths just by simply acknowledging their first amendment right to freedom of speech while deciding not to unduly infringe upon their right to assemble in their respective congregations. I doubt any Southern Baptist will visit a mosque, wear a skull cap and start praying with Muslims just to exhibit their "tolerance" to that person's Islamic faith. The only time a Southern Baptist would engage in such activities is if he/she actually wants to become a Muslim. At that point, tolerance morphs into voluntary assimilation. In fact, it brings to mind the idea postulating imitation as the most sincere form of flattery. If we use this train of logic, it would be felicitous to conclude that most women admire lesbians for their seemingly uninhibited sexuality. Or maybe they admire the mettle of these women for actually admitting to the cognate feelings they may harbor themselves, but lack the guts to aver due to fear of ostracism from family and friends. I would argue these "straight" women who engage in lesbian behavior are the biggest hypocrites who want the benefits of membership (i.e. making out with another woman) without actually paying the membership dues. Essentially, they are like the "trial subscribers" to lesbianism who decide to cancel their subscription when the real lesbians try to get serious with them asking for a commitment. Then they decide the allure of the male part is too compelling to forsake just to become a fully-fledged lesbian. Almost any woman who has been emotionally scarred by a man possesses lesbian tendencies because they subconsciously seek the sentience of other women—the same sentience and sensitivity men supposedly lack. As far as I am concerned, it's just a pathetic attempt to garner attention and subvert yourself from the subliminal reality that you genuinely are a "fence sitter."

70. ***Your only understanding of "experimenting" resonates during Spring Break.*** According to the National Science Foundation in a survey conducted in 2001, only 43 percent of American respondents understood how a scientific experiment was conducted. I am sure that percentage would at least double if you asked American adults the social meaning of experimentation. I am sure many of them would admit to "experimenting" just to eradicate their inconspicuous and clandestine predilection of their own sex out of their system. The only thing more pathetic is the fact you spend thousands of daddy's dollars to enact your wild fantasies on a remote island on the Keys as if your behavior becomes any more palatable when you do it in Florida. If we are discussing experimentation, I would be curious to know exactly what the hypothesis is. Perhaps the hypothesis for the confused heterosexual woman entails the idea that she will still want to be a heterosexual even after dipping into the forbidden pool of homosexuality. I guess all the data collections and observations are collected between the sheets or maybe in a random tape that you consented to even though you were in an inebriated state. The only result that really matters is that you came out of the experience a more confused and obtuse-minded woman than you were before. It's good most Americans don't understand the meaning of the word "replication" as it relates to a scientific experiment or they would expand the "Experimenting" to Christmas (under the mistletoe), Thanksgiving (with a post meal feast), Halloween (nobody would even notice with the costumes), Memorial Day, fourth of July (with indoor fireworks), or even

Labor Day (where they will be busier than any regular business day). In fact, according to a Boise State study (apparently more serious than their smurf turf football field), 60 percent of women reported being physically attracted to another woman. Furthermore, a dating site called OK Cupid (still a little more serious than the Boise State smurf turf) reported that one in three of its female subscribers reported "hooking up" with another female. Yet our society does not view most of these females as even "bisexual" since it's perfectly natural for females to enamor over the beauty of other females. However, a male that engages in the same behavior is categorically labeled a homosexual. I am sensing a fourteenth amendment violation. Oh no, it's just another one of those silly double standards in gender relations we have rolling in America.

71.   ***You blame cigarette addiction on nicotine.*** Nothing irks me more than all these cigarette "addicts" acting like victims because they were asinine enough to start smoking themselves. It is analogous to blaming the fire for burning you when you place your hand directly into it or even the snake when biting you after leaning in for a kiss. Just like it is in the fire's nature to burn you and the snake's nature to bite you, it is in the cigarette's or alcohol's nature to make you dependent on it as it saps the life out of you. There are gargantuan warning labels and multitudinous public health ad campaigns telling you not to smoke and you continue to figuratively and literally play with fire. I never understood what it is about smoking that attracts people to it. Is it the potential of contracting lung and mouth cancer? Is it the allure of the people talking through an artificial voice box since they have a hole through their throats? Is it the putrid smell that stenches their clothing? Is it the pungent sewer smell that protrudes from their mouth each time they breathe? If you have such a fascination with seeing your own breath after puff, perhaps you should move to Alaska where it is cold enough most of the year for you to see your breath each time you exhale. It's time we stopped blaming the movies, music, the cigarette companies themselves (who are ironically advocating against cigarette use), or even stress (since

everyone deals with it and not everyone needs a carcinogen chalk in their mouth to deal with it). It's time we started blaming the buffoons who willfully make the decision to start smoking themselves. It's not as though anyone lodged a gun to their head and coerced them to start smoking. Just like anyone who places their hand on fire or tries to get amorous with a rattlesnake, people who make the choice to start smoking are bona fide oafs. They claim to engage in smoking to cope with stress instead of dealing it with the normal way like working out or eating a box of large pizza from Hungry Howies. Okay, the last technique is not really normal; it's something I do since pizza cheers me up. Essentially, deciding to start smoking is tantamount to a slow and painful suicide. Just like the saying "death by 1000 cuts," smoking is death by 10,000 butts (or how many ever butts it takes to eventually kill a chain smoker).

72. ***You exhibit fanfare of a particular sports team by drenching yourself in paint*** and exposing the entire world to your lard pool of a stomach. Every NFL season during the frigid months of November, December, and January, I see these shirtless white trash fans painting their team's colors on their chests and stomachs. I know their corpulent bodies have an advantage due to extra insulation, but they must have skin made of steel to at least act as though they are impervious to the wind chill factor in some of those Northern cities such as a Boston, Chicago, Cleveland, or NYC. I guess since their brains are impervious to scholarly enlightenment, it's fair their stomachs are resistant to the intransigence of the winter cold. Even if the weather is not considered frigid, you have to commend these buffoons for the shamelessness they exhibit by exposing their seemingly unattractive canvasses in public. It makes me wonder what kind of standards operate at stadiums in the status quo. In any regular establishment in America be it a restaurant, fast food joint, supermarket, or shopping center, you need a shirt to be allowed to stay in the building. I guess vitriolic fanfare is the exception to this rule once again proving the paramount status of sport in America—even higher than decorum or common sense.

73. ***You wear t-shirts with slogans on your chest area*** to force people to lay eyes on your breast area. This ilk of t-shirts is what I would like to call a "sexual harassment bait machine." It's human nature to follow the curiosity stemming from the wandering eyes. Anytime we see a slogan on a t-shirt, it assumes a cynosure role to our eyes and we have a proclivity to actually read the slogan. It takes us a few seconds to realize we are inadvertently staring right into the lady's breasts. Of course the lady catches you red-eyed staring at her breasts and either a)calls you a pervert b) calls everyone's attention to a potential rape c) accuses you of sexual harassment or d) all of the above. It's clear these women strategically wear shirts designed to lure wandering eyes to their breast areas to legitimize their pathetic existence and massage their voluminous egos. Even all the university sweaters these chicks wear have the letters stationed at the breast area.

Random Man: So I see you attend Penn State.
Woman: And you needed to stare at my boobs to get that information you pervert!
Random Man: No, it's just written near the chest area.
Woman: Someone help me, I am being assaulted! This man is trying to rape me!

You know the rest of the story. The man tries to calm the woman down by putting his hands over her arms and the cavalry comes to kick his ass into the Stone Age where an increasing number of Americans are living now inside their minds.

74. ***You take your dogs everywhere with you.*** As a Muslim, it's becoming tougher to walk in public places in this country because you have insouciant owners who release their dogs onto the streets the same way they allow their children to gambol onto incoming traffic. One time, while filing out of the post office in Bryan, TX, I observed an elderly man with a cane who inexplicably neglected to have his dog on a leash. I trembled in terror as I was leaving the post office to the point

where I cowered behind the door to potentially shield myself from a potential attack from the generally bellicose German shepherd. My roommate also drifted to the side and harbored the recreant feelings I did toward the shocking situation. I believe it was an act of God saving both of us from being attacked as the gentleman and his German shepherd casually walked into the building while I sprinted toward the car. It just stupefied me how someone could act in such an inconsiderate fashion allowing their dog to just frolic around like it is an innocuous child. It also irks me to see dogs in the back of pickup trucks or even inside the truck barking away while I am walking toward the store. Is it considered "animal cruelty" all of a sudden just to leave your dog at home unattended for a transitory period? I also get baffled seeing these slot machine skanks bring their little poodles inside the mall from store to store as if they are shopping with their BFF. I never understood why people do not bring their cats with them considering cats are nattier while dogs leave their feces and urine everywhere. Since the number of childless couples are growing (close to 27 million of the 58.4 million married couples in the United States), it's become quite common for these couples to give their dogs this de facto child treatment. They spend thousands of dollars buying their clothes, medications, food, drink, exercise machines, pedicures, manicures, and hair treatments. If only someone decided to open a university for dogs similar to the school for monsters in that Pixar movie, your dog may end up costing more than the child you did not want to have just because children are extraneously expensive. Then again, I am certain most Americans would still want to have dogs instead of children since it would not require teaching the dogs any manners or educating them. God forbid you would have to teach your children how to count, read, and write, especially when you lack competence in these skills yourself. It's time to realize that while dogs are chordates and mammals just like humans, they are not humans. Dogs are animals that need leashes to protect surrounding people from getting attacked by virtue of their fickle instincts. Please stop treating them like humans and allowing them to make non-pet enthusiasts like myself blush every time I step into a public setting at the unprecedented anemic level of apropos present in our society today. States have "leash laws" for a reason: so idiotic owners who allow their bestial dogs to maim innocent people are held liable for their negligence as what happened in San Francisco a few years ago.

75. ***You open up a wedding registry and engage in concomitant temper tantrums*** when others do not pay for your wedding. First of all, the development of wedding registries is as egocentric and self-absorbed of an act as puerile children who pen outlandish Christmas lists for their parents as if they are entitled to everything they want. I guess this callow behavior fails to recede from little girls who nominally "mature" into women after which time Christmas lists are supplanted by wedding registries. According to the slipshod logic of those who generate wedding registries, it is the responsibility of the wedding attendees to pay for your microwave, blender, convection oven, silverware, big screen television, PlayStation 4, robot vacuum, herbal exfoliating treatments, pots, pans, shower curtains, king sized mattresses (to accommodate both of your egos), high efficiency washer and dryer, a year's supply of Omaha steaks, an iPad, an iPod, spa treatments, and Katy Perry concert tickets. Whew, I hope I didn't miss anything on that list! God forbid the Bride-zilla changes her wish list between now and the wedding. The sense of entitlement of these brides is risible to the point where they coerce guests into thinking they are obligated to pay for their wedding. The bottom line is you made the decision to get married and orchestrate a baroque wedding, thus, it's your responsibility to ensure that a)you can afford to get married and b) you can afford the wedding. Instead of asking guests to buy all these luxuries for you, it would be more salubrious to petition the Pillsbury DOugh-bama boy on Pennsylvania Avenue to bail you out and pay for your electricity in the process. Adding another $10,000 to the federal deficit wouldn't hurt that much, would it? Essentially, this is what I feel about weddings coming from an Indian family: you decided to get married, you pay all of the expenses pertaining to the

wedding and its aftermath. Furthermore, if any guest graciously decides to provide a gift (no matter how meager or largesse), accept it with gratitude because they are doing you a favor regardless of what your delusions of grandeur may be telling you. Your guests' only responsibility is to provide moral support by attending the wedding. They are not obligated to even bring a gift, let alone help you pay for the pretentious event.

Of course, there was a vintage case of Bride-zilla at her finest that I perused on Huffington Post (yes I read Huffington Post occasionally, shut up!). A young woman shared a story about her "friend" that got married and had the gall to deliver a scathing review of her "contribution" to the event. The only way I can do this story any justice is to quote the primary source of this overweening jerk of a bride. She sent a message through Facebook (very brave of her) stating the following: *"Hi Tanya, how are you? I just want to know is there any reason or dissatisfaction of Mike's and I wedding that both you and Phil gave $50 each? In terms of the amount we got from you both was very unexpected as a result we were very much short on paying off the reception because just for the cocktail + reception alone the plate per person is $200 (as per a normal wedding range with open bar is about) and Mike and I both have already paid for everything else including decor, photography, attire, etc. and didn't expect we had to cover that huge amount for reception as well. As I know you both live together and work, so I did not see any reason for that amount, when it comes to your wedding hopefully you'll know what I mean. I hope for the best as from what we receive is what we will give back. Anyways, good luck on everything."*

Apparently the guests were expected to cover their own costs for the reception since it's perfectly normal to spend $200 per head on food and wine for an event. For this price, you can attend a grandiose Vegas buffet for breakfast, lunch, and dinner and still have enough money left over to watch the UNLV football team play in Sam Boyd Stadium (sorry Rebel fans, I had to get that in). Perhaps the bride and her mate should have picked a less expensive venue for their wedding because caviar, tilapia, filet mignon, and a pretentious "open bar" are not necessities for a wedding nor is it the responsibility of your friends to cover all the costs associated with your "dream" wedding. It's your dream, thus, it's your responsibility to pursue it and not bring everyone down with you. Now it all makes sense why our brain paralyzes our body while sleeping so we don't act out our dreams. Why can't more women be like Kristen Bell and just spend $142 to get hitched in a court? That way, there are no broken friendships or feelings stemming from an unfulfilled "wish list" you felt entitled to because daddy dressed you up as a princess for Halloween when you were in seventh grade thereby brainwashing you into actually thinking you are a princess whose desires will always get satiated.

76. ***You use the ER for non-emergencies.*** In 2008 (the most recent year of data pertaining to ER visits), there were 124 million visits to hospital emergency departments. Out of these visits, between 8 and 27 percent of them have been deemed "non-urgent" depending on whether you believe the CDC or Health Affairs folks. Furthermore, Rand Corporation reported that "non-urgent" and "routine" use of the ER from people accounts for $4.4 billion of annual health expenses. The interesting part of these findings concerns the fact that people with health insurance coverage comprise the largest portion of the ER abuse for non-urgent, routine care that could be procured cheaper and more seamlessly at their PCP's office. That's right: the assholes with actual health insurance are the ones clogging up the ER while people without insurance are suffering from actual emergencies. Sorry women, thinking you may be pregnant after a casual encounter in which you did not use contraception does not constitute a medical emergency. There's something called a twenty-four-hour pharmacy to obtain the so-called emergency contraception (a.k.a. the magic wand for when I fucked up really bad by not wearing a condom before fucking a random dude in the back of a pickup truck). Sorry guys, a headache or frequent urination stemming from heavy alcoholic intake the night before does not constitute a medical emergency. Sorry hypochondriacs, a cold does not constitute a medical

emergency either. Take some Tylenol, Nyquil, or Dayquil and go to sleep. The most flagrant (to the point of being malfeasant) abusers of the emergency room are the buffoons that use it when they contract a simple sore throat or acute bronchitis. The danger in this situation is the expectation patients hold that the indolent, avaricious physician will prescribe them antibiotics. According to a study at the revered Brigham and Women's Hospital in Boston headed by Dr. Jeffrey A. Linder, (physician and researcher at BWH's Division of General Medicine and Primary Care), their assumption holds profound merit. This study examined the discrepancy between cases requiring antibiotics and the actual prescribing rate in the 39 million visits for acute bronchitis and 92 million for sore throat by adults attending primary care centers or hospital emergency departments. Dr. Linder mentioned two particularly important findings. The first finding he mentioned involved the fact that only 10 percent of people with sore throats contract strep and antibiotics are only supposed to get prescribed when the patient has strep. However, the national percentage of antibiotic prescription for ER patients with sore throat hovered around 60 percent. This means a profusion of doctors are endangering the welfare of their patients by superfluously prescribing antibiotics, which will ultimately precipitate a counterproductive effect by increasing the concentration of "superbug" bacteria. This "superbug" bacteria causes antibiotic resistance in humans which results in extensive hospitalization and death. A CDC study asserted it is responsible for $20 billion direct health care costs and another $35 billion a year in lost productivity. The second finding which I found more disturbing involves the 73 percent prescription rate for ER patients beleaguered with acute bronchitis when the actual percentage should be around 0 percent according to Dr. Linder. In fact, for these conditions, the basic remedy should only involve rest and fluids according to Dr. Barnett (another lead author of the aforementioned study). Thus, this unnecessary use of the ER is compromising the population level efforts to curb infectious diseases since the overuse/over-prescription of antibiotics confers antibiotic resistance. Yet Americans still gravitate toward these antibiotics like they are gummy bears and jelly beans. Perhaps it may relate to the design of these medications and how they appear as appetizing as candy. Never judge a book by its cover unless of course you see Ann Coulter on the cover because you automatically know it will be hideous and obtuse just like her.

77. ***You think condoms are a panacea to any potential STD's.*** According to Jill Grimes (a practicing physician and author of "*Seductive Delusions: How Everyday People Catch STDs*"), condoms do not protect you from STDs that are transmitted through skin contact. These STDs include herpes (not to be confused with slurpies), syphilis (you cannot spell syphilis without P-H-I, right frat boys?), HPV (often symptomless which makes it even more dangerous), and pubic lice (sure as heck makes you want to have sex with a caveman, doesn't it?). According to the CDC (one of the few government agencies that does their job), the failure rate of condoms is 18 percent. That means there is nearly a one in five chance the condom will leak and not prevent the "unwanted" pregnancy or even the equally "unwanted" STD. Not to mention these risks are amplified when you engage in the salacious practice of anal sex. Not only is it an abominable practice if you are a religious person, but it is becoming quite frequent amongst Americans as anything else that is licentious. The most poignant example of the shameless sexualization of American society entails the mention of "Adam and Eve" and how it has vitiated to the point of becoming more known for serving as a site for "sex toys" to satiate the most squalid of fantasies. Ask any couple on the streets who Adam and Eve are and I can say with certainty most of them will rejoinder with a response to the tone of "Oh, they are the patron saints of sex toys" or "They are the nice people who sold us the vibrators and the dildos that have turned our world upside down." Since the US Constitution does not abrogate religious practice (at least not yet), it seems our society has relegated to the tactic of satirizing some of the most sacred religious figures in history.

78. ***You use the term "committed relationship" without being engaged our married.*** I know this will infuriate all the people

out there with boyfriends, girlfriends, or both (in the words of my tenth-grade world history teacher Mr. Davis). One of my favorite shows on television is the scandalous "Cheaters" in which the cases are composed primarily of the following groups: white trash, ghetto blacks, or wannabe ghetto Hispanics. I completely sympathize with the people who are victims of adulterous infidelity because that entails violation of a sacred marital contract. However, when it comes to cheating boyfriends and girlfriends, it's pretty difficult to sympathize with the so-called victims. As long as there is no ring on your finger, you are not in a "committed" relationship. In the "Cheaters" show, the people committing the infidelity often cite the lack of availability of their significant other as the crux reason for their actions. The bottom line is men and women both have internal "needs" that must approach fulfillment. Men primarily want their sensual desires fulfilled. Thus, if you as a girlfriend are not giving your boyfriend the proper physical attention, they will scavenge the market for someone who will satiate their carnal desires. You can attribute it to the stereotypical male pig persona, but that is the reality of the situation to which you need to adjust. As for female, their needs are mainly emotional. They generally want a guy who will engage in active conversation (primarily active listening) and remain emotionally responsive. This involves persistent hugging, kissing, cuddling, and doting in the form of flowers, chocolates, and miscellaneous gifts or thought-provoking gestures. Guess what guys? If you are not "emotionally available," your ladies will find other men who are willing to engage in lengthy "heart-to-heart" conversations over Starbucks Frappuccinos and cuddle at night. They have no obligation to stay in a phlegmatic, nondescript relationship if there are more spry avenues available. It is analogous to the relationship between a restaurant and their customers. If the customers feel the restaurant is not meeting their expectations in terms of service or food, they will survey the market and flock to other restaurants that better fulfill their culinary demands. It is not as though there is a "contract" between boyfriends and girlfriends that require unconditional loyalty just like there is no contract between a customer and a restaurant. These boyfriend/

girlfriend relationships (or even relationships between the gays) evince a strict "give and take" mechanism until of course it morphs into engagement and eventually marriage. Thus, if your boyfriend or girlfriend cheats on you, chances are you assume some degree of culpability for a) not giving your "significant other" enough attention to disabuse them from shopping the marketplace to "see other people" or b) failing to acknowledge the danger of embarking on a relationship with someone who may have a proclivity for philandering. This construes why I chuckle a little bit when I see the term "open relationship" on Facebook because I think all these non-marriage, non-engagement relationships essentially fall under the "open relationship" bucket. Thus, if a guy has a girlfriend and finds out he connects better with another woman, there is no problem if he ends up ditching the former girl for the latter without informing the former. He is not "cheating" on the former girl mainly because he never commenced any significant contract with her in the first place. It's comical how you have Americans who are anorexic toward marriage and play the dating card expecting the dating card to carry the same "exclusive" privileges of marriage. Talk about having your cake and eating it. Get it through your thick heads: dating is for people who do not want commitment regardless of how seriously you are dating while engagement/marriage is for people who want commitment. For the idiots who argue they need ample time to become acquainted with someone, just realize that comes with an appreciable risk of your "significant other" eventually finding interest with another person. Perhaps you do not need to date someone for four years to realize whether you want to spend the rest of your life with them. Kudos to Adam Brody and the pulchritudinous Leighton Meester for fast tracking their relationship from dating to engagement within a matter of five months. The Jew that cannot act bagged a real winner in the "Gossip Girl" belle who will probably serve as his meal ticket once that obnoxious droll charm reaches the empty. The point of the story is simply to stop messing around or else you will be the one getting messed around with in this dilapidated dating arrangement.

79.   ***You have a fascination with bottled water.*** Let's start with some eye-gauging facts. According to the Beverage Marketing Corporation, 9.1 billion gallons of bottled water were consumed in the United States in 2011—an average of 29.2 gallons of bottled water per person. The plastic bottle production concomitant to this bottled water supply requires 17.6 million barrels of oil, which I guess is okay as long as the ragheads comprising OPEC are supplying it to us. Eighty-six percent of these empty plastic bottles are not recycled further besmirching the environment with pernicious chlorine gas and heavy metals as a result of incineration. Okay, I may sound like an ardent environmentalist, thus, I will not belabor the platitudes concerning its harmful effects on the animals because that would require a book on its own. However, I will frame this topic from an economic standpoint to illustrate the fatuousness of the bottled water habit. This can be illustrated by two facts from Riverkeeper–a New York-based watchdog organization that is baffled by the fact New Yorkers continue to drink exorbitant levels of bottled water despite having one of the most pristine water sources in the world contributing to the uniqueness of their famed pizza. The first fact involves the cost of tap water compared to bottled water: the former costs $0.002 per gallon while the latter costs anywhere between $0.89 to $8.26 per gallon. That means you are paying anywhere between 445 to 4,130 times more per gallon for water just because it comes in a bottle. Last time I checked, bottled water does not come mixed with cocaine, marijuana, or that stuff which "gives you wings." Thus, I doubt the practice of spending 445 to 4,130 times more for bottled water comes across as cost-effective. The second fact which exacerbates the sheer stupidity of buying bottled water is that 40 percent of bottled water emanates from the tap. Thus, you are literally paying 445 to 4,130 times more for tap water that's placed in a bottle. Instead of buying bottled water, perhaps it would be more financially salubrious just to fill the finished 20 oz. or two-liter soda bottles with tap water instead of wasting another couple of bucks buying tap water from the store. Better yet, there's something called a water filter that you can buy at a pittance compared to a bottled water

system if in fact you have determined the tap water system in your local area is tainted. The most staggering aspect of bottled water deals with the chemicals associated with the plastic: bisphenol A (BPA) and phthalates. BPA is a known endocrine disrupter associated with a myriad of health abnormalities not limited to cancer, neurological disorders, early puberty in girls (may explain why Miley Cyrus and other young girls took the adage "13 going on 30" literally) and premature labor (might explain the profound increase in children with developmental disorders). As for phthalates, they are related to plummeting sperm count thereby increasing the need to take Viagra exposing yourself to an increased possibility of tomato face along with the inability to distinguish between the colors blue and green making you wonder if the sky is actually falling. In addition, phthalates are also associated with testicular abnormality/tumors, and gender development issues. Thus, the "plastic fantastic" makes more Barbies want to become Kens and vice versa or it may just make them indistinguishable. All joking aside, the central components of the bottled water containers are responsible for the blooming incidence of endocrine and neurological disorders. However, that is just a small price to pay to enjoy the taste of water from a bottle even though it still tastes like water.

80. ***You view wrestling as "fake."*** Yes, wrestling is staged and the results of each "match" are fixed by the writers. However, wrestling is like any other form of entertainment such as soap operas, movies, theatre productions, or sitcoms. It involves sedulous mental and physical training to deal with the workaday rigor of the job. Unlike the aforementioned examples of entertainment, wrestlers endure tremendous physical pain. When they jump off a ladder to entertain the crowd, the pain associated with the landing is NOT fake. When they take a chair shot or get rammed through a table, the pain associated with that impact is NOT fake. When they bleed, it is actually blood and not packs of ketchup they whimsically squirted in their own face. When wrestlers know they will be in a match that requires bleeding, they take quite a bit of Tylenol to

thin the blood and then use a blade to cut themselves. This combination yields effective, grisly, and realistic blood jobs. Wrestling does involve some acting to sell the force associated with dropkicks, clotheslines, shoulder blocks, and other pedestrian moves used through the course of a wrestling match. However, there is still pain associated with taking those moves which once again is NOT fake. The most interesting fact about wrestling involves the ropes that encompass the ring. Those ropes are actually elevator cables that leave ostensible indentures on the body during the first couple of months of a wrestler's career until the body becomes inured to getting "Irish whipped" into those ropes. Thus, the marks on the body and pain stemming from Irish whips are NOT fake. All this accruing pain coalesced with the persistently demanding schedules of wrestlers explains their propensity to use painkillers and steroids at an alarming rate (in Chris Benoit's case, it was ten weeks' worth of anabolic steroids every three to four weeks). For example, wrestlers who work for WWE (the preeminent wrestling organization in the world) are on the road about 250 days a year doing up to four shows a week. Unlike other professions, wrestling does not have an established labor union or organization to alleviate this schedule or incorporate a set of protections for them. Until this happens, you will continue to see wrestlers endure real profound pain with little relief in sight aside from the customary painkillers and steroids. People might argue these wrestlers voluntarily choose this arduous lifestyle and all these adverse events evince a mere comeuppance. That may be true to an extent. People might argue wrestling is an asinine waste of time catering to the lowest common denominator of society. That may also hold true. However, promulgating that wrestling is "fake" is both ignorant and preposterous once you consider the tremendous pain and persistent pressure these wrestlers must perform under on a workaday basis.

81. ***You complain about teams "running up the score."*** In the effeminate au courant American society, it is now considered "bullying" to play your best football for sixty minutes even

if the process requires embarrassing the opponent along the way to victory. Consider the example of the Aledo (TX) football coach Tim Buchanan who was accused of bullying by the parent of the pussycat Western Hills team following the chagrin concomitant with a 91–0 emasculation at the hands of Aledo. Apparently, the pusillanimous parent was disgruntled due to the Aledo coaches' refusal to instruct players to abate their efforts with the outcome essentially decided within the first five minutes of this squash match. I will use a pragmatic argument for the necessity of "running up the score." Let's say you run a company and you have employees who work a fixed schedule of eight hours a day and/or forty hours a week. You would want to get the most out of your employees and that entails an expectation of them working the full allotted time. Even if they completed all of their immediate tasks, you would still expect them to tackle extra tasks to keep them busy. You would not want them to shut it down early or even allow them to go home before their shift ends. You would want to instill a concrete work ethic in your employees by maximizing their productivity thereby optimizing the efficiency of your company. Of course, most Americans know very little about working hard for their full shift as most surf on the internet trolling their friends on Facebook, fishing for YouTube clips as well as their occasional pornography. According to NICE (a prominent analytic solutions company), employees on average waste two of eight work hours and 45 percent of the reported time wasting occurs through internet surfing. Of course, the most reportedly visited time waster was Facebook with 41 percent of the respondents in the study. Unlike many of the hackneyed industries many Americans work in, athletics is superfluously competitive. It requires a persistent commitment to improvement in order to stay at par or above the competition. In the case of the Aledo football coaches, their rationale for "running up the score" is simple: they wanted to reinforce the importance of playing hard from kickoff to the final horn. Anyone who watches sports on a daily basis realizes that big leads get blown in games at all levels due to the team with the big lead taking their foot off the pedal. Laziness leads to sloppy play, which manifests in losses. The Aledo coaches were simply considering the downstream implications of potentially slacking off in a game that seems well in command. It is these kinds of slipshod habits that led to blown leads, thus, it is imperative to foster habits of vigilance and persistent sedulous effort regardless of the score. The bottom line is, there is always room for improvement and expecting competitors to "lay off" when the game is out of hand deprives them from the opportunities they need to test new tactics as well as hone their craft. Then again, it is understandable if you take out your star players in these situations to protect them from superfluous injuries—a lesson learned the hard way by Mike Shula when he kept his star WR Tyrone Prothro in the game during the fourth quarter of an impending blowout win in the 2005 season against the Sally Gators effectively pulverizing their chances of winning a national title when he was lost for the year after fracturing his fibula and tibia. However, even when playing backups, the intent for coaches should be to stay aggressive since they are paid to coach the full game not just the part of the game where their team builds a comfortable lead. "Sportsmanship" is for people not good enough to be champions. There's a reason why a "killer instinct" is the sine qua non of becoming a champion. You do not develop a "killer instinct" caring about sportsmanship and other people's feelings because winning is the only thing that matters at the end of the day.

82. ***You take Adderall/Ritalin despite not having ADD/ADHD.*** For a country that gets all sententious in their crusade against PED users, I am nonplussed as its nonchalant attitude toward academic cheaters in the form of normal people who beseech medical professionals (or their ADHD friends) for the mind-enhancing drug without any actual condition requiring the use of this drug. For the record, Adderall and Ritalin are for people with actual attention or learning disorders. However, students at the University of Kentucky seemed to miss the memo just like the entire football season ever since turning the affirmative action charity case Joker Phillips loose on the program. According to the research of a professor Alan

DeSantis of the University of Kentucky (a.k.a. Fried Cunt-yucky Capital of America), 30 percent of students enrolled in this rarefied institution of higher learning have illegally used a stimulant (such as the aforementioned ADHD medications) while half of all juniors and seniors in the study admitted using them. Furthermore, 80 percent of underclassmen in fraternities and sororities used them so they could party hard for their mandatory social in the middle of the week and pull an all-nighter to maintain their GPA enough to earn another semester of hardcore partying with daddy's money. The 2009 National Survey on Drug Use and Health research ascertained that college students were twice as likely to use Adderall for recreational purposes as people of a similar age not matriculated in a university. I guess the pressure of succeeding in college is cognate to the pressure of athletes succeeding in sports. Trends seem to indicate both groups are resorting to illegal drug use to bolster their prospects of success, yet only one of these groups seems to get ecumenically vilified by the media and on the streets as a "cheater." The bottom line is cheating is cheating regardless of whether it is to hit a few extra home runs, run a few seconds faster, or score a few points higher on a microbiology final that represents the proverbial go-ahead run to drive you into admission at a medical school. There are students who don't use these mind enhancing drugs and rely on conventional hard work and intelligence. These are the students who end up getting shafted by the slackers who resort to using Adderall and Ritalin to obtain an unfair advantage. As a society, we seem content with endorsing the Machiavellian mentality asserting that the ends justify the means except in the case of athletes since we somehow hold them to a higher moral standard as if they are monks. Oh, by the way, Adderall and Ritalin are class 2 drugs with a high risk of dependency and addiction according to the FDA. By turning a blind eye to this blatant turpitude on the part of non-ADHD students taking ADHD drugs, not only are we blurring the lines of morality, but we are setting up our younger generation on the pernicious ride to addiction and other evils of drug dependency. But I guess the ends justify the means even if the ultimate end is rehab or a tragic death caused by an intransigent fight with a controlled substance. If we are going to hold athletes to a certain standard regarding PEDs, we must do the same for our aspiring academicians heading into the same cutthroat world of the job market, desire for promotions, and the quest for a prosperous career. Ultimately, isn't the desire for acceptance and success what really drives athletes to use PEDs or academics to use mind stimulants?

83. ***You cannot start your morning, afternoon, or evening without a cup of coffee.*** Whether you are watching your favorite characters on "Pretty Little Liars" huddled together in a colloquial conversation before class (Okay, I'm guilty as charged for watching that show), sprinting to make it to your 8:00 AM class, or scurrying to your 9:00 AM Monday morning meeting, chances are you will encounter some sort of coffee sipping through ornate brown plastic cups which have rendered the proverbial mugs obsolete. According to the National Coffee Association, 54 percent of Americans eighteen or older drink coffee every day. This group of coffee-drinkers averages a consumption of 3.1 cups a day, which seems to line up with my satiric hypothesis of coffee in the morning, afternoon, and evening. In addition, each cup averages 9.1 ounces of coffee—a little more than the customary 8 ounces that are in 1 cup according the asinine United States customary unit measurement system. Maybe this could explain the spike in obesity and/or diabetes since Americans are drinking more coffee than what should be allowed in an actual cup. That extra 1.1 ounce adds up, especially when you douse the coffee with whipping cream, aspartame laced Splenda (which is more harmful than regular sugar by the way), and cookie crumbs. Perhaps the US Standard units should change the conversion of cups to fluid ounces from 1:8 to 1:9.1 to reflect the current trends of American coffee consumption preferences. All joking aside, you are a bigger TAA if you actually buy into the idea that coffee is salubrious for your health considering it is a known ADH blocker (a.k.a. diuretic) which dehydrates you precipitating more urination breaks

at work. To add further credence to this idea, a University of Alabama study demonstrated that women who consume large volumes of caffeine (a key ingredient of coffee) are 70 percent more likely to become incontinent (which aligns with the increased unwillingness of Americans to travel outside the United States and Canada). Furthermore, a Commonwealth Institute of Health study in Australia indicated a strong link between increased coffee consumption and symptoms such as indigestion, insomnia, and headaches. Isn't it ironic that a drink which people consume to make themselves more alert actually contributes to their inability to sleep properly to begin with? Take home lesson: make sure you do not drink coffee straight out of bed before consuming your bread, eggs, and ham or you will get indigestion. Furthermore, a University of Nevada School of Medicine study demonstrated that caffeine reduces fertility in women by up to 27 percent. I guess that is not much of a problem for Americans since more couples in this country are averse to having children anyway preferring to raise dogs instead. Finally, a Mayo Clinic study determined that men who drank more than four 8 oz cups (apparently some academics still adhere to the idea that one cup equals eight ounces) incurred a 21 percent increase in all-cause mortality. The sooner Americans learn about the vested interests of a certain group controlling the media and how they are linked to a coffee supergiant, the more they will realize the talk of coffee's health benefits is actually propaganda. If you want a healthy drink, switch to green tea, but not the Arizona version lathered with ginseng.

84. *You treat the Super Bowl Sunday like Christmas* even though it is as hackneyed and predictable as an eighties horror movie script. Just like you trick your children into believing the existence of Santa Claus, you have tricked yourself into thinking the Super Bowl is an actual exciting and unpredictable football game. Before the Denver Broncos literally took the "Pot Bowl" to heart delivering a cold turkey performance against the Seattle Seahawks, the Super Bowl was as predictably choreographed as the main event of WrestleMania (a staged

event like all entertainment based wrestling). Ever since Roger Goodell took over as the commissioner of the NFL, the Super Bowl has literally become an entertainment spectacle rather than a football game. In fact, Goodell exudes as much antipathy to football as Vince McMahon does to wrestling as both men have efficaciously effaced the physicality out of their sports emphasizing the entertainment value of their respective brands instead. When it comes to the Super Bowl, there are a few rules of thumb particularly germane to the Roger Goodell era.

The first rule of thumb is the fact that the first half of the game is always nondescript in the sense that it is low scoring and/or one sided. All the Super Bowls in the Roger Goodell Era (circa 2006) fit this description. The Colts/Bears in 2007 was low scoring. The Pats/Giants in 2008 was low scoring despite the fact the Pats had the most prolific offense in NFL history to that point. The Steelers/Cards in 2009 was one sided with the Steelers holding a 13 point lead at the half. The Colts/Saints in 2010 was low scoring (16 combined points at the half with the two best QBs in the game makes one suspicious). The Packers/Steelers in 2011 was one sided with the Packers holding an 11 point lead at halftime and their lead was as large as 18 at one point. The Giants/Pats sequel in 2012 with a familiar ending started off with a drab 10–9 halftime score. The Ravens/49ers was one sided with a 21–6 Ravens halftime lead that swelled to 28-6 early in the third quarter once the power came back to the shithole Louisiana not so super Superdome. Essentially, I tell all my friends who are new to watching football to disregard and skip the first half of the Super Bowl because it usually is a snooze fest.

The second rule of thumb concerns the aforementioned low scoring games magically becoming exciting shootouts in the fourth quarter. The Giants/Pats game involved a combined 10 points in the first three quarters of the game before they bandied three touchdowns in the fourth quarter including the frenetic final drive for the Giants that involved an epic catch by the proverbial "flash in the pan" David Tyree before the real epic catch by Plaxico Burress over the overstretched arms of Ellis Hobbes to give the Giants the lead for good. The Colts and Saints doubled their output in the second half compared to the first half as the Saints magically found their offense scoring 15 points in the fourth quarter (actually their defense scored 7 of those points courtesy of the Peyton Manning pick 6). The Giants/Patriots in 2012 was not necessarily a shootout in the fourth quarter, but it magically manufactured a compelling fourth-quarter finish with another epic Eli Manning TD drive followed by another epic Tom Brady collapse. Gosh it seems to have a similar ring to the game they played in the fourth quarter four years ago. If it were a movie series, I would demand a refund because the second game was essentially a replay of the first game. As the saying goes, it evinced "old wine in a new bottle" with the venue playing the role of the new bottle.

The third rule of thumb involves the games that are one sided in the first half, which inevitably become competitive as the other team makes a furious comeback. In the Cards/Steelers game, the Cards scored 16 unanswered points to actually take the lead before Big Ben engineered a superlative TD drive aided by the Arizona Cardinals D-coordinator whimsically deciding to play prevent defense allowing Santonio Holmes to roam freely around the field. In the Packers/Steelers game a couple of years later, the Steelers cut the once 18 point deficit to 3 points in the fourth before the Packers added a FG to swell the lead back to 6. The Steelers had a chance to win the game in the final minute, but a fourth down pass from Roethlisberger to Ward fell haplessly incomplete. However, this still fits the pattern of the trailing team spearheading a fierce comeback attempt. Just last season in the Ravens/49ers game, the 49ers were trailing by 22 points early in the third quarter after a Jacoby Jones kickoff return. However, they reeled off 23 of the next 26 points of the game and had a chance to win it in the last minute, but failed to convert on fourth and goal from the Ravens 8 yard line.

The fourth rule of thumb is that you should pick the less hyped, underdog team to win the Super Bowl. Including this year's Seahawks triumph over the Broncos, the underdog has won 6 of the last 7 Super Bowls. The only exception was the Cards (as a 7 point underdog) losing to the Steelers after pulling ahead with less than two minutes to go despite spotting the Steelers a TD late in the first half when the Cards were about to score themselves. Essentially, it took quite a bit of fortuitous bounces (and calls) for the Steelers to buck this trend. Some might argue this representing hindsight bias, but it seemed to me the Broncos were doomed when Peyton Manning decided to accentuate his focus on doing Papa John's commercials (and promoting their free pizza promotions once you sign up for Papa Rewards) than actually learning how to dissect the sweltering Seahawks defense. His lack of focus and preparation were pretty obvious in quite possibly the most inept performance by a QB in Super Bowl history as he only guided his team to a total of 8 points while throwing two INT's and losing a fumble. Not to mention the fact that he gave up a safety allowing the ball to go over his head and another pick 6 on the second interception he threw. Thus, he scored as much points for the other team as he did his own. It did not help he needed 49 passes to throw for 279 yards—many of which came when the game was out of hand anyway. Calling him overrated is an insult to the word "overrated."

The fifth (and most important) rule of thumb entails the Super Bowl being the most overrated, elitist, and predictable waste of time out of all the championship games in major sports. According to Greg Johnson of the *LA Times*, 25.2 percent of the tickets to the big game are controlled directly by the NFL. The process of obtaining the tickets for an average Joe is dilapidated in the sense that you cannot buy them directly from a ticket office or an online marketplace like Ticketmaster. You have to send the NFL a certified letter between February 1 and June 1 of the year preceding the Super Bowl you wish to attend in which one drawing is only allowed per address. Afterward, a random drawing/lottery is held for the honor of buying the highly overpriced tickets which averaged a low of $2,862 for the "Pot Bowl" according to Jeane MacIntosh of the *NY Post*. Otherwise, they generally cost an arm and a leg however much those run at in the au courant atmosphere of profound economic crisis. I have a feeling the NFL would not accept arms and legs as a payment unless of course they can be fitted on the past players who have literally lost an arm and leg playing in a league that is content with throwing them on the streets without any compensation. All joking aside, I think it would behoove you to spend money on better games like the BCS National Championship game where you see passionate fanbases and players clashing for school pride rather than mercenaries who are using this game to leverage a better deal in order to abscond to another franchise after the season is done. Trust me: the *L* in NFL does not stand for loyalty.

As a disclaimer, people might counter my arguments concerning the Roger Goodell Era by bringing up the Colts/Bears Super Bowl as well as the Seahawks/Broncos game. In all fairness, the Seahawks/Broncos game did fit the banal description of a one-sided first half. The only problem is they did not make their inevitable second half comeback mainly because Peyton Manning was still thinking about his next Papa John's commercial and how he plans on promoting the revolting cookie pizza. In both situations, the weather was far from ideal. The Colts/Bears game was a rainy mess while the Seahawks/Broncos game was far from balmy as the temperature hovered around 50 degrees Fahrenheit all night. Thus, these two games deviated from the aforementioned patterns quite possibly because the weather deviated from the typical peachy/controlled conditions of a Super Bowl game. I rest my case that I have catalogued the Super Bowl down to a science and the science seems to indicate the Super Bowl should be renamed the Super Hole because it is an insult to the game of football and the way it should be played.

85. ***In cold weather, you bundle up at the top and still wear a revealing skirt at the bottom.*** When I lived in Boston, this

trend never ceased to baffle me. I got excited about the cold weather because I thought the sorority row of street tramps would actually put on some clothes for a change. However, they just dressed like high-priced hookers with their furry coats, short skirts, long socks, and high boots. They may feel comfortable at the top, but I cannot imagine how the brisk Boston winter winds would not reach their legs and make them feel discomfiture. Then again, it seems logical to conclude they have become desensitized to the concept of pressure building up on their legs as they voluntarily allow other people to open them up for meat inspection. I would hate to be a vice cop in cities like Boston because virtually every girl in that city dresses like a hooker or a tramp to the point where it becomes impossible for them to conduct their job without turning into door to door salesman. Of course, the women represent the doors in this metaphor. It's quite interesting many of these same girls end up contracting colds or other ailments due to this weather. Perhaps it has something to do with the fact you did not bundle up on the bottom half of your body. When I attended BU for graduate school, the area around the BU Medical School gained notoriety for rapes as the School of Public Health circulated as many as three emails during one of the semesters informing students of rapes that transpired in the area. In each of those emails, they mentioned how the female victim walked alone in the dark alley near the medical school in the wee hours of the morning before getting apprehended and raped. I do not mean to palliate the occurrence of rape, but I would venture to say walking alone in a dark alley late at night dressed in a trendy provocative manner reeks of categorical stupidity. Nobody deserves to get raped, but at the same time, nobody deserves to get burned by fire even when they are dumb enough to put their hands into the fire. I think the focus on psychology in the contemporary world should shift the focus away from the mind of sociopaths and toward the minds of these tarts that render it felicitous to dress like Gina the Beach Warrior only to sport indignation at "undesirables" who possess the gall to peek at the spectacle they have made of themselves. Please, American ladies: put on more clothing not only for your own health, but just so you can save some face and possibly demonstrate that your IQ is at least above the normal monkey range. Otherwise, you will be subject to the persistent "chick or treat"-ers that treat every night like their Halloween with the only difference being that both options are savory.

86. ***You celebrate your mother for one day as if it excuses the brazen manner you treat her the other 364 days of the year.***
I contend the most ostensible characteristic of this deteriorating American culture involves the callousness in which the society seems to treat mothers. When I look at how children (especially daughters) act toward their mothers at a supermarket or anywhere in public, it seems as though they genuinely believed they did their mother a favor by allowing their mothers to give birth to them. I will utilize television to expand upon my argument since television provides the most accurate lens upon which to assess the downtrodden state of American values. Let's start with America's favorite guilty pleasure "Keeping Up With the Kardashians." It is abhorrent to see the kind of invectives the three effete Kardashian sisters launch toward their mother every episode. It is appalling enough to utter the word "fuck" in front of your parents regardless of the context, but it is especially distasteful when you tell your mom to "fuck off" or point blank utter the words "fuck you." There was even a time when Kourtney (the Cinderella of the trio of tramps) asked her mother "Are you fucking retarded?" when she misunderstood what Kourtney said over the phone. Even Kim Kardashian's ex-hubby felt repulsed by the way Kim talked to her mom forming one of the myriad of reasons they eventually broke their marriage after a lengthy seventy-two-day ordeal. I know Kris Kardashian may evince the living version of Cruella Deville without the half blonde hair and with a daughter (Kim) who has probably slept with over 101 men taking the place of the actual 101 Dalmatians. However, even the most cynical person can see the enormous sacrifices she makes on a workaday basis for her kids only to get treated with contempt. Another example can be seen in all the "Housewives" shows, particularly the one in New Jersey with the way daughter Ashley talks to her

mother and one of the main characters Jacqueline Laurita. I watched a few episodes where not only does Ashley talk back to her mother incessantly, but she refers to her mother as a "bitch" right to her face. I cannot think of too many things more repulsive than essentially likening the woman who gave birth to you to a dog. Even if you watch many of the popular sitcoms like "Two and a Half Men," "How I Met Your Mother," "Broke Girls," "Hot in Cleveland," "Modern Family," and "Melissa and Joey," all these shows portray characters in some form or another who resent their mothers and view them as a nuisance. The mothers are always portrayed as overbearing, insensitive, condescending women who are responsible for everything wrong with the main characters themselves. I remember one episode of "How I Met Your Mother" when the character Robin (played by the smoldering hot Cobie Smulders) was talking to her mother on the phone essentially ignoring her the entire time and chiming in every couple of minutes sarcastically uttering "Well you can blame dad for that." 'Modern Family" is the best example of how little respect is given to mothers as neither of the daughters Hailey or Alex really respect their mother Claire as they persistently mouth off and disobey her along with persistently barraging her with condescending remarks concerning her fashion sense and eccentric personality. In turn, Claire essentially carries on the rivalry with her own mother as those two bandy one another with subtle jabs concerning the décor of Claire's house and the drinking habit of Claire's mother. Basically, the callousness and brazen attitudes displayed toward mothers in these shows represents a microcosmic view of the unapologetic irreverence displayed by Americans toward their mothers in actual American society. The most egregious example can be seen in the reprehensible "16 and Pregnant" show on MTV where you have teenage girls engaging in "unwanted" pregnancies with the expectation their parents will raise their babies. These same brats possess the shameless gall to act in an abrasive fashion toward parents who graciously allow them to stay in the house despite their indiscretions of giving birth out of wedlock while still in high school. It is just repulsive how much Americans take their parents for granted and then view them as a nuisance when it comes time for them to take care of their parents due to deteriorating health. I wonder if most of these people actually realize this woman known as their mother kept them in their own womb for nine months and endured the vastly excruciating pain to bring them into this world. It's like Americans are brainwashed into believing that childbirth is not much of a task at all. Neither is changing diapers, feeding, clothing, waking up in the wee hours of the morning tending to fickle cries, getting them ready for school from K-12, and actually raising them to become somewhat independent. With one day where we buy them threadbare Hallmark cards, hackneyed roses, and discounted chocolates, all the disrespect in the world hurled toward mothers seems to get effaced. Honestly, I think Mother's Day is an insult to mothers worldwide because they should be celebrated for their inordinate sacrifices every day throughout the year. One day is not enough to engage in pretentious celebration in the form of burnt waffles and trite cards hollow of meaning written by spurned English majors who moonlight as erotic phone sex partners. Why not give your mother a kiss, a hug, a thank you, or even a simple "I love you" on a daily basis to demonstrate that her efforts are genuinely appreciated? Let's face it: none of us can actually ever repay our mothers for their perpetual sacrifice no matter what kind of gifts we bestow upon them when we obtain considerable wealth. Yet we seem content deluding ourselves with the perceived apropos of mocking our mothers every day for the entire year except the magical Mother's Day when we conveniently decide to actually treat our mothers like humans rather than zombies. However, it is nice to see sentient young women like Ariana Grande who know how to treat their mothers well outside of Mother's Day. There are two cloying tweets which underscore the unexceptionable love she possesses for her mother. The first tweet emanated from the time where Victoria Justice's fans reportedly made her cry at an autograph signing. Afterward, she disseminated the following message on Twitter "Wish I were more like my mom. She's such a bad ass, I'm such a mouse." Amazing how someone with a lofty status in show business can still humble herself in comparison to her mother. The second tweet came in response to an encomium delivered on Twitter in which her mother asserted the following: "Just heard my daughter on a conference call. Quite a businesswoman! Can't say idk [I don't know] where she gets it from." Ariana Grande promptly responded with a succinct statement saying "I get it from my mama." It's amazing how she took time out of her busy schedule to simply acknowledge and display gratitude toward her mother. Most girls today would fall into a paroxysm if their mothers mentioned them on Twitter even in a positive light. Awesome and rarefied gals like Ariana Grande do give me a slight ray of faith in America's ability to appreciate their mothers until of course I witness the television networks glorifying the "Italian mother-daughter rivalries" through the sordid *Housewives* shows. Perhaps Ariana Grande should get a reality TV show of her own to show all the spoiled TAA girls and entitled tarts how to treat their mothers with respect outside of a specific Sunday in May.

87. ***You keep coining meaningless "National" days to squander money, expand your waistlines and inveigle your way to acceptance.*** Examples include National Cats Day (If your name happens to Cat, Kat, or some version of Catherine, this day is not for you), National Dogs Day (if your name is Bill, George, or Barack and you have served as a US president at some point in the last quarter of a century, this day is certainly for you to celebrate your ancestry), National Doughnuts Day (a.k.a. cops get fatter, dumber, and slower day due to the sugar drain accompanying this superfood), National Boss Day (since we all just love our bosses as much as our furry electricity bills), Sandwich Day (relevant for any married man smothered between his quarreling mother and wife), Magic Day (to appreciate our resident scam artists), Valentine's Day (to celebrate Jessica Biel and Jennifer Garner releasing their frustrations on the piñata), Beer Can Appreciation Day (seriously, this is a designated day to appreciate bacchanalian behavior and lack of recycling of the cans), Barbie Day (since

she seems to be the inspiration for the "Plastic Fantastic" frenzy pervading American women), Pig Day (perhaps this should supplant Thanksgiving since most Americans are more grateful for their pork than their parents or anything they conveniently claim to be "grateful" for during a day they are consuming large helpings of turkey), Porridge Day (as if anyone voluntarily eats porridge anymore), X-ray Day (yay, let's celebrate exposing ourselves to unnecessary radiation), and best of all, Monkey Day to celebrate the quotidian "reverse evolution" of many Americans back to monkeys as more of them fail to properly write a five-paragraph essay or locate New York on a US map. If you peruse the Days of the Year website, you will see mention of hundreds of other meaningless days commemorating the activities that either makes us obese, depressed, asinine, delirious, or some combination of these characteristics. Valentine's Day satisfies all these requirements. They should really consider combining Police Day, Pig Day, and Doughnut Day since police officers are pigs that love doughnuts. You can't top this 3-in-1 special that would even put the famed Trinity to shame. Unlike the Trinity, it actually makes sense perhaps because it is not literally suggesting 3=1.

88. ***You nonchalantly call each other "dog"(or "dawg") while engaging in colloquial dialogue.*** When I was growing up as a middle schooler and subsequent high-schooler, I observed the interesting behavior of black people as they persistently referred to each other by the canine appellation. "Yeah, dawg, I was at Keisha's house and I spanked that ass so hard that Big Ben came out of the clock tower and asked for my secret." "Naah, dawg, I ain't got no money to pay you. Let me hit you up tomorrow dawg." Pretty soon, the term "dawg" to address friends started getting utilized by Caucasians, Hispanics, and even Asians. I know American society essentially views dogs in regal fashion as evident by the incessant shameless promotion of the 2014 Westminster Dog Show resulting in 3.719 million viewers on the same night as the State of the Union address where another dog disguised as a US president attempted to edify the public about the state of the country.

However, I would hope people realize that humans are a little bit more advanced intellectually than dogs and are considered higher order primates. Thus, it should be viewed as an insult to call someone a "dog" since it means they are less than a human. I guess it is only an insult when a man calls a woman a homologous form of that word since women seldom engage in paroxysms similar to that of a dog's barking. Furthermore, this asinine adoption of a bestial African American vernacular cultural custom further illustrates the growing propensity of most Americans flocking to the ribald lowest common denominator like a moth to a flame. Other examples of this behavior include our fascination with relatively vacuous rap music which contains nothing of concrete cultural value aside from glorification of cursing, crime, drugs, alcohol, premarital sex and womanizing. It's insulting to the wider African-American culture when you consider the perception of African-American culture is shaped primarily by narcissistic buffoons like Jay-Z, Kanye West, Drake, Lil Wayne, and J. Cole rather than transcendent work from gifted artists like Michael Jackson, Ray Charles, Louis Armstrong, Duke Ellington, and Charlie Parker. As a society, we seem content to limit our understanding of African American culture to obtuse vernacular rhetoric, baggy pants, and rap music. There is a more resplendent and illuminating side to African American culture which edifies us about their struggle for freedom and acceptance—two concepts most minorities in contemporary America take for granted. In most other parts of the world (including my country of origin India), being called a "dog" is considered an insult naturally because people do not want to be associated with the sordid, disruptive, and hostile creatures with the crooked tails. Somehow in America it's considered acceptable unless of course you use it toward a woman. Then you get transferred to the line for sexual harassment lawsuits. I wonder how much of this phenomena can be explained by the fact most Americans seem to approach life with the same insouciance and subservience as dogs. The insouciance is construed by the penchant to only eat, drink, play, fuck, sleep, and push the repeat button. The subservience manifests in the stupefying trust in government and the lack of desire for intellectual inquiry to bring scrutiny onto the government's normally wild arrogations as a disguise for their underhanded behavior. In a perverse way, Americans might be justified in referring to each other as canines due to the indubitable veracity associated with this characterization. However, most Americans evince the worst kind of dog: the one that just barks, but fails to deliver any bites.

89. ***You "study" for a test rather than learn.*** When I matriculated at Florida State during my undergraduate years, I encountered a finicky (yet polite) chemistry professor of German descent whose name I will not state since he might contact the Anti-Defamation League to sue me for describing him as finicky. He made a comment about American students that I will never forget when he stated, "You Americans seem keen on studying for exams rather than actually learning." In my estimation, his caustic comment could not describe the reality of the American student more felicitously. American students approach their education, classes, and learning with an "ad hoc" attitude. This entails just learning the information for the class and forgetting it afterward only to get burned when they actually need to remember it again. Much of American education is designed to transform students into robots. The "Why is this important" and the "How can I apply it" has essentially vanished into oblivion getting supplanted by threats of failure as well as feelings of chagrin if one does not memorize the correct sequence of all 50 US presidents on their next test. When focus of education gets placed on memorization of novel stimuli, it operates to anesthetize the intellectual curiosity of the student. When I took trigonometry in my second semester of college, I was appalled at how many students did not remember how to use the basic Pythagorean Theorem that should have been learned as early as Algebra 1. Even when I tutor students online for Brainfuse Incorporated, I encounter Algebra 1 students who do not understand rudimentary principles such as the distributive property, ratios, multiplying and dividing fractions, percentages, how to find

a reciprocal of a fraction, or even the order of operations. I went to public school in Tallahassee and I learned the freaking order of operations in third grade. Most students take algebra in ninth grade, and they essentially struggle with concepts they should have learned as early as third grade. It does not mean they are stupid as much as it indicates the abject failure of our education system to properly foster an atmosphere of sequential learning for students. In math, science, and even English subjects, information functions like a building which starts with a strong foundation lending its way to continuous development to the top. Essentially, this means you cannot expect to run a marathon when you cannot even walk properly. Another comical example of the "ad hoc" manner in which American students approach education involved organic chemistry 2 lab when the professor promulgated that some students said "I had no idea I still needed to know organic chemistry for this lab." Well, the purpose of any lab is to apply what you learned in class, but you would not know that if you were not a college campus based on my experience at FSU. Then again, I can't really blame the students so much because all of the focus on organic chemistry classes at FSU centered on memorizing structures and reactions without any mention of the relevance behind learning these structures or reactions. One time during the lecture, a student asked the professor the real life application of the Diels-Alder reaction. The professor responded by asserting "I don't know, but I do know you need to know it for the test." When a PhD level organic chemistry teacher does not know how to explain the relevance of a reaction, you wonder if anyone really cares about education anymore in its puritanical form. It's almost like education has dwindled down to a fashion in which people obtain their degrees with little practical knowledge/skills associated with the degree in the field which they earned it. Then again, I have to give Kourtney Kardashian some credit as she earned a degree in "Drama" at the Zona and proceeds to utilize those skills in sprucing the action on "Keeping up with the Kardashians." Otherwise, according to Jaison Abel and Richard Dietz of the Federal Reserve Bank of New York, only 27 percent of college graduates hold a position germane to their major in college. I'm not berating these people, but it just provides further corroboration to the idea of the college degree transforming into an ornamental fashion rather than anything substantive.

90. ***You debate abortion in a public setting.*** The debate of abortion must be the most trite, otiose, incendiary and woefully predictable disquisition in the history of mankind. There has never been an abortion debate that sparked anything useful aside from hostility, resentment, and political mudslinging. If you are a religious person, you think it is tantamount to legalized murder. If you are a liberal, you think it is the woman's right to choose the course of her body. Debating this topic in terms of convincing the other person to change their stance is as fruitless of a venture as if a group of Red Sox and Yankees fans convoked and tried to convince the other group to change sides. However, what people fail to realize is the ruling behind *Roe v Wade* actually tried to mediate both of these considerations. People think the case advocates for a woman's right to abortion, but in reality it just states the government cannot interfere with the woman's right to procure an abortion. Thus, the government does not have to necessarily pay for the service nor does it need to make the service readily available. In addition, the government can institute a twenty-four-hour waiting period to ensure the patient meaningfully exercises their right of informed consent. However, the government cannot place an "undue burden" that woefully diminishes the woman's ability to procure an abortion. Examples of an "undue burden" include mandating parental or spousal consent—both of which are understandable if the parents are brain warped Catholics or if their "significant other" is physically abusive. The most egregious aspect of *Roe v Wade* is not anything within the ruling as much as how the ruling is perceived by the "conservative" dimwits in the Repub-Lycan Party who have probably never read the ruling. I am a conservative Muslim who actually thinks *Roe v Wade* evinces a sound ruling based on concrete Constitutional principles. Now if you despise *Roe v Wade*, it must mean you detest the US Constitution.

Thus, it may be time to find another country to live. Perhaps you can ship off to Iran or Saudi Arabia where abortions are abrogated and women probably receive the death penalty for even requesting one. Even the so-called Christians do not understand what their own book says about abortions. I would like to see a Christian or a Catholic find me the portion of their holy texts stating that a woman victimized by rape must carry the baby to full term. When I think of Christians (and Catholics), one line in the Qur'an seems to suffice in construing their behavior when it states "they are like donkeys carrying tomes." In Islam, the woman is allowed to procure an abortion if they have been raped, if the pregnancy poses a viable threat to their health, or if they might be too old to endure a pregnancy. Wow, that sounds very oppressive to me compared to the donkeys (oops I meant Christians and Catholics) who force their women to carry out a pregnancy despite circumstances outside their control such as someone raping them. Back to the main topic at hand, abortion is a complex topic that should not be viewed from a black and white camera lens. Yet it remains a black and white issue to the extent that people cannot discuss it civilly. Perhaps there should be a law interdicting its mention in public places because it is as alluring as breastfeeding in public.

91. ***You are proud of being "tolerant" of people who are different from you.*** According to Merriam-Webster dictionary, the denotation of tolerance entails "willingness to accept feelings, habits, or beliefs that are different from your own." The manner in which the word "accept" is used in this context is rather vague. Moreover, if we try to define "accept" using the Merriam-Webster dictionary, we are further flummoxed since accept can mean "to give admittance or approval to" or "to endure without protest or reaction." As we surmise from real-life, the former definition of "accept" probably does not work in the aforementioned denotative context of the word "tolerance." This is because you cannot possibly give approval to "beliefs that are different from your own" nor can you approve contravening "feelings" or "habits" in the same fashion.

As for the latter definition of "to endure without protest or reaction" that does not seem to apply either in workaday settings particularly talk show radios since protest and/or reaction accompanies every display of "feelings, habits, or beliefs different from your own." Thus, my issue with the word tolerant lies in its blatant vagueness that further obfuscates the prospects of divergent parties meaningfully embracing their differences. Instead of "tolerance," it would behoove us to preach understanding. The word "tolerance" is as futile and rudimentary as the word "potential" in describing the skills of a child. "Oh, even though you are failing algebra, I feel you have the "potential" to become a rocket scientist discovering life on Mars." When you fill the child's mind with delusions, you are not doing them any favors. Instead, you are depriving them of the opportunity to acknowledge their own special skills and traits which they should hone to maximize their genuine (rather than perceived) potential. Similarly, when you preach "tolerance," you are just allowing people to take the path of least resistance rather than imploring them to learn about different cultures. To this day, there have never been any adverse effects stemming from learning about different cultures and celebrating diversity. In fact, this multicultural society formed the underpinnings that propelled America to the top of the new world order. It's the celebration of diversity which compels luminaries from around the world to migrate to America to contribute to this former "Melting Pot." Basically, the word "tolerance" is another example of the ineffectual rhetoric stemming from the indoctrination of the "Political Correctness Act." It's just another circuitous way of avoiding the problem thereby generating a steeper divide between people of different races. In chapter 49 verse 13 of the Qur'an, Abdullah Yusuf Ali translates it as the following: "O mankind! We created you from a single (pair) of a male and a female, and made you into nations and tribes, that ye may know each other (not that ye may despise (each other)." The operative set of words here is "know each other." The Qur'an does not preach tolerance, but it actually goes a step further in terms of preaching understanding of people different than you.

Most Americans do not understand why Muslims abstain from food, drink, or sex from dawn to sunset during the month of Ramadan. They equate fasting with masochism, but that tune may change if they realized fasting was prescribed to promote self-discipline and empathy for the workaday struggles of the indigent who generally go without access to drink and food in most parts of the world. When I edified many of my friends, peers, and acquaintances of this fact, most of them learned to respect the custom since they finally understood the meaning behind it. If you do not understand the rationale behind a custom or activity, you are in no position to meaningfully "accept" or even judge it. To utilize a more secular example, let's consider the American aversion to soccer and the rest of the world's aversion to American football. If both parties actually considered the underlying factors surrounding the appeal of the respective sports, they might appreciate its appeal. For example, soccer is considered a "universal" sport due to its simplicity in the sense that all you need is a ball, your feet, and an open field to play the game. For much of its history, soccer appealed to the masses and served as a pastime for the working and middle class people in both Latin America and Europe. Thus, it evinces a centripetal force that unites people of all social classes and ethnicities to convoke and enjoy the spectacle of such a simple sport. Football has served an analogous role in America for the middle class youth as it also entails a simple game requiring only a ball and an open field. Of course, if you want to play in an organized league, you will need a little more than just the ball and an open field. However, football has always been the sport of choice even in farm, rural and inner cities across America because it represents a blue collar sport that has always appealed to the gritty working/middle class American. Notice that most football players at the college and pro levels came from socioeconomically challenged backgrounds. In short, both soccer and football have always appealed to the values of the masses yet they are centripetal forces that unify people from all walks of life in a country. No matter what financial or personal hardships people in America or any other country face in their lives, they always find solace in watching their favorite football or soccer team play. If both parties actually tried to understand the other's passion for their respective sport, they might realize the commonalities underlying each other's passion. The vitriol Americans display for football is exactly the same as that of Latin Americans/Europeans for soccer. The underlying forces buttressing each respective fashion are also parallel since each sport simply appeals to their respective masses and effectively unify people of divergent backgrounds. In précis, I can confidently conclude that learning about different cultures not only augments our understanding of the world around us, but it also provides further edification of our own values. We may actually realize our culture is not as different as other "foreign" cultures as learning about these cultures hones appreciation of our own. In other words, maybe seeing Manchester United fans paint their faces red and sing through the course of games might make us feel a little normal even after dressing like pirates with spiked helmets doused with gallons of face paint that takes a few days to fully remove. Next time you feel like "tolerating" the foreign couple that moved in next door, choose understanding instead because you may learn a thing or two in the process about their culture and your own.

92. ***You still do not know the difference between their, there, and they're.*** The rumor is that for every ten minutes you spend reading comments on Facebook, you lose an IQ point due to the desensitization of your mind to the incessant errors pertaining to the most basic homonym distinction of the English language—the distinction between their, there, and they're. "The rave is over their tomorrow and there inviting many bands that will be rocking. I know they're will be alcohol over there and I am excited there going to use their fake IDs to smuggle it into the party for us." Of course, it does not help that Microsoft Word cannot descry 67 percent of the errors involved in the usage of the three homonyms. Type the following sentence into Word and you will see that only one of the three errors are detected by the Grammatik of Word: "There coming to see whether there is any ecstasy available over there at the rave." I guess the lack of ability to distinguish

between the proper use of these three homonyms touches upon the aforementioned idea concerning the "ad hoc" nature to which most Americans approach education. The whole idea of learning these basic English skills is so you could learn how to write essays, papers, reports and even memos later in your life without looking like an uneducated buffoon. An example of such rarefied use of the English language takes place in the bastion of all intellectual activity in America named Louisiana. Here is an excerpt from their civil service site (*http://www. my.jobs/alexandria-la/engineer-intern-applicantengineer-intern-1engineer-intern-2engineer-3-engineer-4/43686364/job/*) for an engineering job posting:

"ØSpecific information about this job will be provided to you in the interview process, should you be selected. However, there is no **guaranteed** that everybody that applies to this posting will be interviewed. ØYour application status can be checked online. If your status reads that you have been **place** on the **eligible's** list; **that means that** your application has been forwarded to the hiring supervisor."

It makes you wonder if anyone in Floozy-ana ever learned how to distinguish between the past and present tense in using verbs. Someone could have also used a course or two on how to use punctuations and how not to overuse the word "that" every 3–4 words. Keep in mind someone with an actual college degree putatively wrote this job listing instead of a monkey. Then again, I'm sure a chimpanzee could have formulated a more coherent listing than these idiots from the armpit of America named Louisiana (a.k.a. Lois Lane-ia). This derelict writing confusion amongst Americans forms the central reason why English will never get renamed "American" regardless of whether ignorant Americans actually think they propagated the language of English to the status of a lingua franca.

93. *You contend a little bit of pot is innocuous.* Along with the propaganda encompassing the arrogated health benefits of coffee, Americans are being bombarded with more spurious

propaganda regarding marijuana (a.k.a. Mary Jane a.k.a. pot). As of this moment, two states legalized personal consumption and possession of marijuana (Colorado and Washington). Over twenty states have legalized use of pot for "medical" reasons. As a preface, I will concede marijuana consumption is a complex issue considering many of the studies concerning the long term effects of it are inconclusive. However, the known facts pertaining to marijuana entail its association with the following adverse short-term effects: impaired short term memory, difficulty thinking or problem-solving (further compounding the ineffectual education system's inability to help in this department as is), anxiety attacks or feelings of paranoia (further compounding a teenage girl's perception of being corpulent and the concomitant anorexic urges), impaired muscle coordination and judgment, increased susceptibility to infections (not so peachy when you neglect to wear a condom) and dangerous impairment of driving skills (manifested by the exacerbation of the already anemic attention most Americans give to traffic signals and braking time already). I understand the "health" benefits of using marijuana to deal with the pain stemming from cancers or chronic illnesses. However, marijuana is a known immunosuppressant that actually augments susceptibility to infections and certain types of cancer while curbing the ability to fight cancer through chemotherapy. According to a study in the *European Journal of Immunology* headed by Dr. Prakash Nagarkatti from the University of South Carolina, marijuana triggers the release of MDSCs (myeloid-derived suppressor cells). Basically, these kinds of cells are heavily present in cancer patients and the researchers of this study postulated these cells contribute to the suppression of the immune system in response to chemotherapy thereby proliferating cancer growth. Isn't it quite ironic the wonder drug that putatively ameliorates the pain of cancer patients actually suppresses its ability to fight cancer? Thus, not only does marijuana pose potentially pernicious short term effects, but it also compromises the body's ability to fight cancer and various infections. I fail to see the actual affinity toward marijuana and why people assiduously fight for its legalization. There exists no scientific study that demonstrates its benefits even slightly outweigh the risks. In fact, the so-called benefits seem to engender greater risks to the point where one must consider the iatrogenic effects of marijuana. I almost forgot to mention marijuana's potentially deleterious effects on the heart. According to the National Institute of Drug Abuse (NIDA), marijuana increases the heart rate by 20–100 percent shortly after smoking. Furthermore, marijuana smoking after the first hour is associated with a 4.8 times greater risk of a heart attack. As for the misguided idea insinuating marijuana not being addictive, the NIDA estimated that 9 percent of marijuana users become addicted, 17 percent of those that start as teenagers and 25–50 percent of those that use daily. Just like many other drugs, there are withdrawal symptoms reported by long-term users such as irritability, sleeplessness, decreased appetite, anxiety, and drug craving. To quote Forest Whitaker's character from "Street Kings" when speaking to Keanu Reeves character about his drinking problem "You know the thing they say about vodka and how you can't smell it? It's all bullshit." I feel the same way about the propaganda being spread through the media and popular culture that marijuana is not addictive, especially when you smoke it through a bong. According to the 2011 SAMHSA Drug Abuse Warning Network, there were close to 2.5 million Emergency Department (ED-not to be confused with the other ED afflicting older men and potentially Derek Mo-Rose) visits related to drug misuse or abuse. Marijuana use comprised 18.5 percent of these visits at a rate of 146.2 visits per 100,000 people. Keep in mind this nearly doubles the rate of ER visits attributable to heroin use. I am not suggesting marijuana is worse than heroin from a personal health standpoint, but it sure seems to result in more holistic societal problems as indicated by the ER visit data. Worst of all, the NIDA taking marijuana during pregnancy contributes heavily to elevated risk of neurobehavioral problems in babies leading to the aforementioned issues of compromised attention, memory, and problem solving ability. The CDC reported a 42 percent increase in the number of children being diagnosed with ADHD from 2006–2013. I wonder how much of this surge can be attributed to the persistent visits to the portable pot-ty. Legalizing marijuana ecumenically will only exacerbate the mental health issues in this country particularly that of the ADHD spike. Anyone with half a brain can ascertain the risk to reward ratio of marijuana is close to 1000 to 1. Then again, if smoking and alcohol consumption are legal, why not make the less pernicious marijuana legal as well, right? After all, Americans want to cling on to their first amendment right of being ignorant to the facts and flushing their lives down the cannabis pot-ty.

94. ***You give these sententious preachers the time of day.*** I have to admit the most enthralling aspect of my undergraduate experience involved the Bible thumping preacher oafs who stood in the middle of the student union blasting their titanium vocal cord speakers of hate speech which reverberated across the campus. I was always amazed at how these trolls attracted voluminous crowds based on the wicked insinuations disguised as the word of the Bible. I commend the preachers in the sense they attempted to espouse "values" on a student body relatively bereft of values. However, if they were actually sincere in their cause, they would have invested in a psychology class or two describing the phenomena of "psychological reactance." Basically, if you use threats or effrontery to convey your message, that will further entrench rebellious behavior from the group whose behavior you are trying to change. During my Social and Behavioral Science class in my Master's program at BU, I ascertained that psychological reactance explains why most public health campaigns end in abject failure because they only accentuate the negative consequences of drugs rather than focusing on positive aspects pertaining to abstinence of drugs. Essentially, the "positive" frame always works better than the "negative" frame. If you want further proof, look at the efficacy of the Febreze commercials and how they emphasize "cleanliness" and "freshness" rather than bombarding you with consequences of dirtiness. In the case of the preachers, they chose to promulgate the message that everyone who drinks

alcohol, fornicates, or smokes (insert sinful drug here) will go to hell with no possibility of forgiveness. Admittedly, I agreed with their messages concerning the seamy images perpetuated by the popular media depicting women dressed in tawdry fashion as specious evidence of gender equality. One cannot roam a supermarket in the United States without exposing themselves to a laundry list of sexually suggestive magazines near the cash register displaying a myriad of women like slot machines. On the other hand, the Bible (unbeknownst to most of the cherry picking popular culture prostitute Christians in America) emphasizes the concept of forgiveness for sins, especially when one actively seeks salvation. The preachers at these college campuses are derelict in mentioning forgiveness instead resorting to disparaging remarks about the effete culture. The problem with this approach entails the fact that most people will develop an "all or nothing" mindset when it comes to faith. Since the preachers tell people they are damned to hell for their actions, there exists no incentive in altering behavior due to their impending ominous fate regardless of the adjustments they choose to make in the course of their life. Obviously, the purpose of these preachers is to instigate furor from the masses and promote animus rather than promote the authentic message of the Bible. The most effectual way to eradicate these trolls involves persistent denial of their existence in favor of proceeding with your daily activities. Even if you desire to counter troll them, you only fall deeper into their trap thereby giving them credibility. At FSU, I witnessed several overzealous students verbally and physically accost these preachers to the point of landing in peril with the police officers. I only nodded my head in disbelief as to why any sensible person chose to give attention to these ersatz preachers risking jail time in the process by getting superfluously involved. Thus, when you choose to embroil yourself into an argument with an idiot, you eventually transform into an idiot yourself. Then again, we are talking about FSU students: it's quite possible they were already idiots before deciding to trade barbs with the resident preacher buffoons. It may just serve as an example of a law in chemistry postulating that "like dissolves like." Now we wonder why the Westboro Baptist Church continues to get more portly and disruptive in their efforts. When you issue petitions on the White House website calling for a rescindment of their non-profit exempt status and form counter-demonstrations to their processions, you only fan their flames of antipathy while bolstering their credibility. Then again, Americans find affinity toward idiots like moth to a flame. In America, we have freedom of ignorant hate speech, but we also have the freedom to ignore ignorant hate speech. Perhaps it is time to invoke the latter right.

95. *You play fantasy football.* According to the Fantasy Sports Trade Association (Yes, there is an official organization linking all the cuckoo clock tower stat crunching couch potatoes living in their mother's basements), there are 25.8 million people in the United States playing the monstrosity known as fantasy football. This moniker may have been more felicitous if it got used to describe the aspiring playmates playing football in their lingerie, but they got beat to the punch by the fighting Rotisseries legitimizing their lives by fake owning the jocks that picked on them in grade school. Seriously though, fantasy football has morphed into a disease plaguing both the hearts and minds of actual sports fans. Instead of cheering for a football team, most football "enthusiasts" find themselves cheering for players on both teams in a game. Here is a typical conversation with a fantasy football junkie at a sports bar:

Me: So are you cheering for the Broncos or the Patriots?
Fantasy football fan: Well, I have Peyton Manning on two of my teams, Tom Brady on one of my teams, Shane Vereen on another, Rob Gronkowski on all my teams and the Broncos defense. I need them all to play well.
Me: So are Tom Brady and the Broncos defense on the same team?
Fantasy football fan: No. They are on separate teams, but I do need Tom Brady to throw TD's to Rob Gronkowski since I have him on the same team as the Broncos defense. But I also need the Pats defense to get a few turnovers, but still

allow Wes Welker to get his catches since I have both the Pats defense and Wes Welker on one of the teams.

Me: So who are you cheering for?

Fantasy football fan: I told you I'm cheering for Peyton Manning, Tom Brady, Shane Vereen, Rob Gronkowski, Wes Welker, the Broncos defense, and the Patriots defense.

Me: I meant what team are you cheering for?

Fantasy football fan: All of my fantasy teams of course! I play in premier keeper leagues that cost $500 each. However, I did buy Fantasy Sports Insurance for like $50 for each team. Looks like it will be coming in handy since Rob Gronkowski has been injured most of the season.

Me: Okay man, I hope all your players come up big and all your teams win. By the way, I'm a Titans fan.

Fantasy football fan: What fantasy portal is your Titans team on?

Me: You know what? I have to leave. The Titans game is not showing at this bar. Good luck with your teams.

In a way, I do not blame more fans for not having an actual team to cheer for since NFL since the *L* in the NFL does not stand for loyalty. Unless you live in or hail from an actual NFL city, it does not seem to make much sense to ardently cheer for a team as much as a star player hailing from your college football team. It's amazing how many people in the Bay Area became Colts fans after Andrew Luck got drafted by the Colts in 2012. Even many of the residents of Waco, TX burned their Cowboys flags in favor of the Redskins after they drafted RG3 (a.k.a. Robert Griffin III) who lifted the local Baylor Bears to national prominence after their chronic battle with perennial impotence. Since players change teams as rapidly as RNA virus mutation, there is not much nostalgia involved in the professional football game anymore hence the moniker for the NFL as "Not For Long." It seems like the game gravitates toward individual players more so than the teams. The question is not about the identity of America's team, but about who is America's best QB. As noted earlier in my spiel concerning the Super Bowl, the focus on the NFL has shifted toward entertainment and revenue rather than the quality of the product from an actual football standpoint. Now that the NFL has shifted its marketing to emphasize individual players, the fans responded by just cheering for players via fantasy football rather than cheering for makeshift professional teams. However, this defies the essence of competition since an unwritten rule of spectatorship requires that you cheer for one of the teams in the competition, not the freaking players unless you are a parent with a child on both teams. Football is only fun to watch when cheering for a particular team to win rather than cheering for a QB to throw a TD, a running back to rack up yards, or a defense to force turnovers. There are some people (including a few of my closest friends) who have an actual favorite NFL team and cheer for players competing against that team on a given Sunday (or Monday or Thursday). Seems like a dilemma and a conflict of interest as far as I am concerned. A true football fan would suspend concern of their fantasy team for the more exigent desire of seeing your favorite team win. However, fantasy football has prompted putative Patriots fans to cheer for Wes Welker, putative Jets fans to cheer for Tom Brady, putative Bears fans to cheer for Aaron Rodgers (don't laugh: it happens more often than you think), putative Ravens fans cheering for Ben Roethlisberger to rape (sorry, I meant carve up) opposing defenses, putative Raiders fans to cheer for Peyton Manning and worst of all, putative Cowboys fans to cheer for RG3. It's time for Americans to take their fanhood back and ditch fantasy football before your only favorite teams are the fake ones you spent $250 to make in your artificial leagues. It's almost as pathetic as getting married to someone you met online and falling in love over instant messages. Fantasy football is analogous to the cyber relationship: it's just not as good as the real thing, especially the sex.

No instance illustrates the obtuse nature of fantasy football more than the pastiche ghetto ruffian who utilized his Twitter account to issue a death threat to an apparently hypochondriac Brandon Jacobs sitting out a regular season Monday night game against the Minnesota Vikings. He sent two tweets when he thought he taw Bandon Jacobs being a puddy tat. The first tweet read as follows exactly as the petulant buffoon wrote it: ON LIFE BRANDON IF YOU DON'T RUSH FOR 50 YARDS AND 2 TOUCHDOWNS TONIGHT ITS OVER FOR YOU AND YO FAMILY NIGGER. On his second tweet, he wrote "FULFILL MY ORDERS STATED IN THE PREVIOUS TWEET OR THAT'S YO LIFE BRUH AND IM NOT PLAYING." I have to give this child some credit on being specific as to what he wanted Brandon Jacobs to accomplish that night. He probably did some math and realized he needed a specific number of points stemming from fifty yards rushing and 2 TDs to catch the other loser he is "coaching" against in his fantasy league. However, the fact that he resorted to issuing a death threat against him and his family over a fantasy football league brings into question his understanding of reality. Is a little gold star at the end of the week or bragging rights over your friend really worth threatening human lives over? I am not suggesting this instance as typical of the vitriol of fantasy football owners, but the fact that some fantasy owners are capable of issuing death threats over a team they fake own is disconcerting. Fantasy football is not like gambling where you have to pay a bookie if a certain outcome fails to curve in your favor. At the most, you lose the initial investment you placed into the league if your team's season runs amuck. This instance just proves that if you are dumb enough to play fantasy football that does not involve some form of lingerie, then you are clearly dumb enough to take it seriously to the point where you deem it necessary to ruin or threaten someone else's livelihood. Fantasy football is okay when done strictly for fun, but once the hobby metastasizes into livelihood, you really need to contemplate getting a real life. Even if your fantasy team wins a league championship and you award yourself an iron skillet as a trophy, it still does not top the feeling of seeing your favorite professional team hoist the Lombardi Trophy. Then again, since I'm a Titans fan, I will probably never witness that moment outside of a Madden video game—at least as long as Jake

Locker is the QB. In the meantime, I'm just waiting for Jemeis Winston to get drafted by an NFL team in a couple of years so I can start cheering for that team as my favorite since the NFL is all about the players now rather than the teams. Since Jemeis brought the crystal trophy back to Tallahassee, he has become my favorite athlete of all time sans Barry Sanders. Hopefully Jemeis Winston will serve as the reason I resist the temptation to succumb to the evil fantasy football craze pervading America as trenchantly as the urge of American families to transform themselves into the traveling Kardashians to a bedroom near you. That is once he stops stealing crab legs from Publix.

96. ***You leave a ballgame early when your team is winning (or even if they are losing) just to "beat the traffic."*** There are two polar extreme examples I want to expatiate upon to illustrate the asinine nature of this behavior. The first example emanated from game 6 of the NBA Finals when several fans notoriously left the game with about half a minute to go amidst the apparent impending reality the Spurs were ready to win the NBA Finals on the Miami Heat home floor in a cognate manner as another Texas team two years previously. However, the Miami Heat rose up with a 6–1 run in the last half minute to force OT and eventually seal the victory on an acrobatic block from Chris Bosh on a potential game tying 3 point attempt from Danny Green. Following the game, Chris Bosh requested for the fans that left game 6 early to stay at home for game 7 due to their turpitude. Whether the fans actually heeded the fitting advice is another story, but those same fans tried to reenter the building once they ascertained their beloved Heat forced OT. However, their attempts were rebuffed as per the conditions listed on the "fine print" of the ticket (in both English and Espanol) mentioning that reentry is not allowed after egressing the premises. Even if the Spurs sealed the deal, why not stay until the proverbial bitter end to applaud your team for another remarkable season? Keep in mind there are 14 NBA cities that did not even get to watch their team play in a single playoff game. Keep in mind there are two more fanbases (Bucks and Lakers) who watched their team get swept in the

first round of the playoffs meaning their teams did not win a single game during the playoffs. Keep in mind there are twenty-eight other teams that failed to make the NBA Finals and ten teams that have never reached the NBA finals in their history, but the Miami Heat accomplished this feat three years in a row. The term "fan" is short for fanatic, but there is nothing fanatical about a fanbase who refuse to stay the entire game of an NBA Finals series and display deserved gratitude for a superlative team who allowed them to indulge in a rarefied experience. Unfortunately, this cantankerous attitude from fans has become pervasive across all sports, particularly when their team is on the shorter end of the scoreboard. Think of how boorish it would appear if you left a theater performance after the second act, a movie theater halfway through a film that appears boring, a college class lecture midway, or even your child's (notice I do not say "daughter's" since Americans are now encouraging their sons) dance recital twenty minutes early. Not only are you wasting money by failing to enjoy the full experience, but you are neglecting to appreciate the arduous effort the performers placed in preparing for their respective performance regardless of your perception of its quality. Even if a movie is laggard in the first hour, it might pick up in the climax, thus, making you look fatuous for paying $15 to only watch the boring first hour. I will admit myself as guilty of a similar offense when I attended a Cornell vs. Harvard football game in 2010—a game I had little interest in attending aside from the fact that my Chinese friend (whose name I will not disclose) asked me to accompany him in order to provide him with a live pragmatic field education concerning the rules of football. Since I do not care about either team, this evinced a perfect opportunity to explain the rules of the game without getting superfluously immersed into the actual game. Predictably, the first three quarters of the game proceeded in a lackadaisical manner as the score read 10–3 Crimson over the Big Red. This prompted my friend and me to head for the exits early in this seemingly meaningless and nondescript game between the two Little Red Riding Hood schools. The ensuing afternoon, I decided to check the final score to see if the two teams actually decided to conjure a few more points before the snooze fest hit the triple 0's. I became stupefied after learning that both teams combined for five touchdowns in the fourth quarter after scoring an anemic 10 points collectively over the first three quarters. Harvard won the game by the score of 31–17 in a game that might have driven a few bookies (if any exist for meaningless Ivy League football games) crazy with the over/under nightmare scenario generated with the unexpected fourth quarter surge. Anyway, this scenario illustrated the exigency of watching the entire game due to uncertainty of what could transpire in the final half, quarter or even minute of any game.

On the other end of the spectrum lie fans who exhibit ingratitude even during their team's triumph. A perfect example of such fans is the tree killing bibulous buffoons at Alabama whom legendary Coach Nick Saban chastised for filing out early during home games. Saban took the words right out of my mind when promulgating the following: ""I've talked about players playing for sixty minutes in the game and competing for sixty minutes in the game. And in some kind of way, everybody that chooses to go to the game should stay there and support the team for the game." Perhaps Alabama fans should take notes from Kansas Jayhawk basketball fans who watch their team's games all the way to the final buzzer regardless of how lopsided the score may read. You can hear the dulcet sounds of the crowd chanting "Rock Chalk Jayhawk" to exhibit pride of their team's performance. It evinces the most bone chilling chant in all college sports. Perhaps Bama fans should start their own chants to demonstrate appreciation for the fact their team is a bona fide powerhouse instead of leaving early to catch their toilet paper raids and keg parties on campus. On another detour, when I attended the BC/FSU game in 2010 which resulted in a predictable FSU thrashing of the Bald Chump Eagles, the most memorable aspect of that experience was witnessing the indubitable loyalty of one of their elderly alumni fans. I traded barbs with the guy earlier letting everyone know the direction of the scoreboard, but I grew fond of this gentleman. Even though his beloved team was getting pummeled late in the fourth quarter, he was 1 of 10 BC fans in the entire stadium that stayed to support their team until the acrimonious ending. Then he edified me on the fact that his generation always emphasized staying in the stands until the clock hit the proverbial triple zeroes out of respect for the team. I began to ask myself when these concrete values started dissipating from American society. Now Americans behave like children on Christmas morning who gleefully unwrap all their toys and gadgets only to get bored of these same possessions within a week demanding a new form of entertainment. Now most of them lack the discipline to stay put for 2–3 hours to cheer for a winning team. It could be worse Bama fans: just look down the road in Birmingham in the shithole named Legion Field where garage bands draw larger crowds than the UAB Blazer football team who cannot win more than two games a year nor can they keep a coach longer than two years.

97. **_You immerse yourself into countless hours in front of the computer in role playing games_** such as World of Warcraft, Dungeons & Dragons, and League of Legends. To preface this discussion, I will focus primarily on World of Warcraft (a.k.a. WOW) because Dungeons and Dragons is literally played by people who live in their parent's dungeon dreaming of a time when dragons existed. As for League of Legends, one of my best friends plays the game and it forms the core reason why his indolent ass neglects to read one of the scripts that I wrote loosely based on his own life story.

Let's start with the good news (rare in the au courant America): in 2013, it seems like people woke up to the reality concerning the cancerous nature of WOW to the point the game's user base plummeted by 14 percent from the previous year with a net loss of 1.3 million subscriptions according to gaming publisher Activision Blizzard. When you have a Wikihow paged devoted to edifying readers on "How to Break a World of Warcraft Addiction," you know the game is tantamount to a drug addiction in its destructive nature. Some of the most risible "techniques" mentioned by the people at Wiki included admitting you have a problem, setting up parental controls, giving away bags, eradicating your character, and my personal favorite imploring them to "Do activities that are productive in the real world, but allow you to have the same satisfaction of leveling up like getting fit, learning to cook, succeeding in school courses." These people should really think of going into the therapy business because that advice evinced nothing short of epic brilliance. Based on the techniques advocated by the Wiki writers, one would think WOW addiction is a love child between a cigarette (giving away bags in the form of packs) and pornography addiction (since it requires setting up parental controls and ditching your online erotic dating site character). In terms of convincing the buffoons they have a problem, it might take a lost job, a second mortgage, repossession of their vehicle (which they probably would not realize for a few months since few of them step outside their residences anyway), and an avalanche of eviction notices outside the front door for them to steer the wheel into reality. The biggest dorks amongst the WOW clan are the ones that spend time in an abandoned park area reenacting their memorable raids as if they are partaking in an actual theatre production. I guess we now understand the underlying reason why people become WOW addicts: they are geeky theatre rejects that failed to make it in acting, but want to act out their fantasies on a portal with similar rejects.

This topic strikes a personal chord with me since a friend of my aforementioned friend Sharif essentially flushed his future down the toilet through his abysmal addiction with WOW. I will keep this acquaintance's name anonymous not only to avoid potential legal pitfalls, but out of sensitivity for his current predicament for which I sympathize. This individual possessed tremendous intellectual acumen and seemed like a proverbial "chip off the shoulder "off his psychiatrist dad and accountant mom. His life took a nosedive with a DUI, but he took concerted steps to restore order before plunging into the darkest of holes in WOW. Like an eloquent raconteur, he dabbled about horror stories of people whose addiction to the game forced them to quit their jobs and take loans from the bank just to afford the monthly payments to continue playing WOW (yes, there is a paid subscription for this game unlike most other sensible games which are free and persist on advertising revenue alone). Ironically, unbeknownst to himself, his experience with WOW quickly morphed into a zombie film in its own respect. He stopped attending his classes and even dropped a couple of courses because his life submerged completely 20,000 leagues below the sea of normal human intelligence. Then he failed the remaining courses in the semester predictably as he chose to attend his mandatory "raids" in favor of the mandatory lab sessions for one of his biology courses. In fact, my friend Sharif and I were wondering whether he actually engaged in any concrete action aside from playing WOW. We stepped into his apartment one day and saw a two-month-old Jimmy Johns drinking cup in which the sucrose from the drink started seeping into the cup. In addition, he looked like a member of the Duck Dynasty as it appeared he forsook shaving altogether during that period. Long story short: five years later, his parents kicked him out of the house following several bouts with rehab for "hard drugs" along with a violent episode where he threatened the lives of his parents requiring police intervention. I am not postulating the culpability of his wayward behavior falls squarely on the shoulders of playing WOW. However, the game does have a propensity to hypnotize people into a certain mental vortex concentrated around their PC desiccating their concrete life ambitions in the process. Once an individual egresses from their addiction to the game, they are likely to plunge into more addictive behavior to obtain the same adrenaline rush the game previously gave them. There is a reason the game received derogatory sobriquets such as "World of Warcrack" and "the cocaine of the computer games world" as asserted by the Youth Care Foundation. If I could make an inference from the aforementioned case study of an acquaintance, it seems like WOW preened and desensitized him to plunge into the world of crack and cocaine for a similar fix. If he could overcome a WOW addiction, crack and cocaine don't seem like onerous agents. Basically, people who spend several hours daily in front of computer screens playing fairy tale characters to boost their self-esteem and give themselves a sense of purpose in life should receive a reservation in the next installment of the Diagnostic and Statistical Manual of Mental Disorders. The name of the classification for this group of chronic losers should read "Virtual Reality Dependence Syndrome." For the causes, they could write "Being a loser, being dropped on the head one too many times as a child, social ineptitude, intellectually incurious and sexually anorexic." It seems like all these characteristics are coincidentally pervading the youth in American society prompting them to plunge into addictive behaviors such as hardcore gaming.

98. ***You are willing to pig out in an "All You Can Eat" style buffet at a rundown restaurant*** because you think it is a value based purchase. I understand the fascination with a buffet concept in which you pay a flat price to indulge in as much food as you can fit in your voluminous stomachs. Aside from the fact the American stomach seems to provide further evidence to corroborate the first law of thermodynamics, buffets provide a live demonstration of an inflation that unfortunately does not result in a boom or a pop. However, in some of these buffet place, you may witness the use of a defibrillator in case the heart goes on overload following the exorbitant intakes of salt (from all the crunchy trans-fat laden fried chicken, French fries, meatloaf, and mashed potatoes) neutralized by high intakes of sugar (from guzzling down carbonated beverages since that is the ideal way to hydrate your body after drenching it with all the salt content from the Dead Sea). An interesting insight was provided by Shawn Smilie who is the Executive Chef at the Buffet at Aria in the buffet capital of the world (Las Vegas) during a "Reluctantly Healthy" session hosted by the spry Judy Greer. Smilie asserted one tactic utilized by most buffet restaurants to dupe customers entails purposely placing the starchy and processed foods at the beginning of the line. Not only are these items relatively cheap, but they fill people's stomachs faster. Consequently, people will exhibit reluctance to tap into the more expensive, fresher, and healthier items such

as the fruits, vegetables, and whole grains. Coming from an executive chef of a major buffet (albeit he claims these tactics are not used at his particular buffet), it's clear buffets are money pits designed to suck you into eating unhealthy and cheap food ensuring they will churn an immense profit off your asinine food choices. Superficially, they seem like economically stout ventures until one really delves deeper into the logistics behind the pricing whether it is $5.99, $9.99, $15.99, or even $49.99 (like in Vegas). The bottom line is most people woefully fall short of these respective prices in terms of the food they consume because they settle for eating items that cost the restaurant a pittance. If people actually started eating their fruits and vegetables at a restaurant and flipped those stations rapidly, those buffets would start hemorrhaging cash. However, nobody visits a buffet to eat fruits and vegetables instead opting for food that catalyzes their possibility of a heart attack in the near or distant future. Aside from symbolizing a money abyss, buffets represent a health hazard zone in terms of the bacteria since food is exposed for long periods of time at inconsistent temperatures. Not to mention the cross contamination issues stemming from several people handling the serving utensils at the station fertilizing food borne pathogens such as the Campylobacter (not for skinny dipping), Listeria Hysteria, Salmonella (not a new ice cream flavor from Ben & Jerry), Clostridium (not afraid to come out of the closet) and E. Coli (not eco-friendly). Granted, these issues will likely not surface in high-end buffets like the ones you see in Vegas, but not many buffets in America meet the standard for "high end." The Chinese panda buffets or even the buffets at KFC in Podunk Town USA will likely not foster hygienic buffet practices in terms of ensuring proper food station temperature, especially when you factor in the anemic levels of intelligence and/or regard displayed by the employees of those establishments. Don't turn your stomach into a microbiology experiment: say NO to buffets unless of course you visit Vegas since the food is epic.

99. *You plaster your body with tattoos* all over your arms, legs, stomach, neck, and butt. By this time, you may view me as

a nefarious love child between a martinet Asian father and a Jehovah's Witness mother since I have advocated for an end to everything that Americans find alluring. Actually, I have not advocated for an end to it as much as I'm just pointing out the folly of such behavior. Anyway, nothing illustrates American psychopathy more ostensibly than our fascination with tattoos. According to the Harris market research firm, one in five Americans obtained a tattoo in 2012. First of all, I wonder how many Americans realize the ink from tattoos is generally permanent unless of course a secret society utilizes some esoteric laser technology that reliably (and painlessly) removes tattoos without making it feel like childbirth or castration. Seriously, if anyone could invent such a technology, it would be tantamount to the effect generated by the advent of anesthetics. Otherwise, people will continue to face the proverbial buyer's remorse once they plaster the name of a significant other on their body only to break up a few weeks or so later or even after the inevitable event of a divorce. Not only will the legal proceedings get expensive in the latter, but the emotional toll will become more onerous knowing that you will spend the rest of your life looking at the name of someone on your arm who ended up sucking you dry literally and figuratively. I just hope none of the dozens or hundreds (possibly thousands) of men Kim Kardashian shacked up with conjured enough stupidity to plaster her name on their bodies unless of course they assiduously searched for their next South Korean supermodel with the surname of Kim.

Aside from the inherent masochism associated with the procedure, the FDA recently issued profound concern stemming from an outbreak of non-tuberculosis *Mycobacteria* (NTM) due to contaminated tattoo inks. This should not be confused with Geicobacteria since that only seems to infect lizards and the mind of people who think it is salutary to spend fifteen minutes on a phone to save up to 15 percent on car insurance. Specifically, the FDA raised concern over the *Chelonae* strain linked to infections of the skin, joints, lungs, internal organs, and eyes. It might sound like a bologna sandwich doused with some exotic blend of cheeses, but these infections requires ridiculously long treatment plans. This makes sense once you consider the fact tattoo ink penetrates past the top layer of the skin making the body susceptible to skin infections that trickle down into the joints and internal organs. Also, it is not as though the rough tumble bikers making the tattoos in these rundown shacks follow the most hygienic procedures to sterilize the ink. Just like any procedure involving insertion of foreign material into the body, it requires stringent regulations in terms of sterilization, inoculation, and concrete safety precautions. Many states are beginning to enforce more robust regulations pertaining to aspiring tattoo artists, but there are some states like Wisconsin only require the person update their vehicle registration, fill out an application, and send $60 for a one-year license. Basically, the process is strikingly similar to the mail order law degree business at FAMU along with a course on how to use Wikipedia to write a law review. Moreover, tattoos involve significant risk of bodily harm with no real benefit to the body aside from the emotional satisfaction of desecrating one's body with asinine and "abstract" symbolism. The most disconcerting aspect of tattoos involves the frequency in which professional athletes and other lionized individuals of society flaunt them. It exposes the hypocrisy of organizations like the NBA and NFL when you censure or fine athletes for "unprofessional conduct" such as wearing a pair of socks that do not match, failing to wear a tie and suit for a postgame interview, adorning patches not previously sanctioned by the league on shoes or jerseys honoring a deceased friend or family member (sorry Ryan Clark), wearing a black mask (sorry Lebron James), wearing an unauthorized hat for an energy bar company (sorry Wes Welker) or wearing green shoes (sorry Marshawn Lynch: it was not Tree Hugger Week like every week when you lived in Berkeley). These organizations justify their fines by citing the responsibility of athletes to function as role models for society. However, no fines are handed out for players who display the most obscene (and potentially offensive) symbols tattooed on their body for the entire world to see. What kind of message are you sending to the youth when you tacitly advocate for painful, permanent and potentially infectious procedures to the body? This kind of behavior gives children the ammunition to argue with their parents about obtaining tattoos since their role models on television are getting them. It is similar to the subliminal messages sent to the youth through television when their favorite characters are depicted as inebriated, getting high, smoking, or cursing. In that case, you have parental controls based on content ratings to shield their children from the pernicious effects of television. However, who is going to shield them from the rebellious behavior being glorified on the hardwood or the gridiron when watching their favorite athletes? When the NBA or NFL takes it upon themselves to regulate the behavior of their players under the guise of caring for community standards, perhaps they should promote professionalism by the way of limiting the display of tattoos from their employees. If you work in any professional work environment, the presence of tattoos is considered unprofessional, thus, most people find ways to conceal their tattoos. Perhaps these professional sports organizations should advocate for their players to conceal their tattoos as thoroughly as possible. I always found it equivocally reprehensible when Tim Tebow was prohibited from displaying Biblical messages on his eye black, yet many athletes are allowed to openly display tattoos of the cross on their bodies while they are playing. Last time I checked, nobody has ever received an infection from a Biblical message on an eye black or even from an eye black in general. Maybe our priorities as a society are getting flushed straight down the toilet into the gutters eventually landing in the cultural abyss.

And last, but not least

100. ***You curse out repo men/ women and tow truck drivers*** because of your own stupidity. One of my favorite shows on television was the recently cancelled "Operation Repo" on TruTV. The most alluring aspect of the show entailed laughing at the numerous instances of TAArific behavior where these

idiots resorted to the most desperate behavior to retain their cars. I understand this show was not entirely realistic, but it served as a "reenactment" of real-life events which means as much as Hollywood producers who contend their production as a depiction of real-life events. Fittingly, the show emanated from Los Angeles delineating its propensity for sensationalized and overdramatic sequences. However, one aspect of the show always depicted accurately involved the sheer stupidity of Americans and how stupefied they act when their car gets magically repossessed following multiple months of delinquent payment. If you cannot make your payments, there are other outlets available such as negotiating with the finance company to lower the payments. In addition, you could appeal to the finance company for forbearance or a deferment payment if you lost your job or are facing financial hardship. In the real world, this skill is called communication, but Americans tend to run away from their problems thinking they will eventually blow over and disappear. Well, some things disappear such as your house, your car and your dignity once you lose everything to the finance company or the bank. The worst part of the show entailed seeing the barrage of insults hurled toward the repossession agents when they are simply doing their job. The repossession agents did not encourage you to cease making payments nor did they tell you to neglect all communication with the finance company. Yet you treat them like diabolical vermin when the true vermin lies in the reflection when looking into a mirror.

The treatment is even more egregious for tow truck drivers who have to deal with people needing a remedial English course. For some reason, many Americans do not seem to comprehend the sign above a parking spot reading "Reserved Permit Parking: Violators will be towed at owner's expense" nor do they comprehend the sign that reads "Maximum thirty-minute parking: Violators will be towed." When the sign uses words like "reserved" or "permit," it means you need clearance to park in the particular spot in the form of a decal. Yet, some impetuous idiots who want to make it to the bar in time for

"Happy Hour" forget the fact they lack a decal to legally park in the spot as if nobody will notice. Billy Bob's note to self: Don't park in thirty-minute parking spot during "Happy Hour" since the car is likely to get towed while I'm halfway into my drinking game before heading back to work with my pair of shades. I will admit tow truck drivers are vultures, but they need to make a living just like anyone else. Thus, they prey on morons who do not read or comprehend the warning signs in a parking zone and wait for them to carelessly park in an area most convenient to reaching their final destination. My personal favorite entails the idiots who park in a handicap spot without a handicap permit thinking they will make it back in time before the tow truck drivers absquatulate with their cars. A basic unwritten rule of life is if you break the rules and get caught, the blame lies squarely on your shoulders. However, the manual of the American sense of entitlement has convinced people it is okay to upbraid everyone else for your own poor judgment and concomitant shortcomings. Ergo, even though you parked illegally or exceeded your maximum parking time and got towed, the real culprit is the tow truck driver doing their job. In many ways, the tow truck drivers are performing a public service by clearing spaces for people with permits following the rules as well as people with a legitimate handicap condition and accompanying tags. They also safeguard us from the idiots who park in an illegal and dilapidated fashion occluding other people from leaving a parking lot. If you want a paradigm and most creative display of this inconsiderate behavior, view the parking lots of any mosque during Friday prayer. You will see people parking directly behind the cars parked in designed parking spaces. You will also see people parking in the middle of the lots as if they are issuing a naval blockade. Indeed both tactics prevent the legally parked folks from expediently returning to work. Often their plight is compounded by the illegally parked people hanging around the premises like porch monkeys instead of removing their dead weight vehicles. Unlike most other establishments, the people operating a mosque NEVER call a tow truck to remove the illegally parked vehicles thereby failing to provide any deterrent to such cantankerous behavior. The rationale for mentioning the example of the mosque is to simply illustrate that tow truck drivers prevent public parking lots across the country from looking like a landfill of aggregated cars all trapped in a log jam. Without tow truck drivers, people would park in a reckless and inconsiderate fashion (like they do in a mosque during Friday prayer) further exacerbating the commute back to the domicile life. Furthermore, people will continue aimlessly parking their cars like they hurl their garbage in the public dumpster without stern repercussions for their behavior. Thus, tow truck drivers promote compliance of acceptable parking laws and standards through punitive measures attacking the wallet (and dignity) of transgressors. I was on the receiving end of a few tows while at FSU, but I realized my culpability in each situation since I parked illegally while in a hurry to make it to class. I took a risk and incurred the ramifications of illicit parking. If people took responsibility for their actions, they would learn from their mistakes in a more facile manner. However, plastered throughout American society are leaders who have a propensity to deflect blame to subordinates or external factors rather than accepting responsibility for their blunders. A team typically follows the behavior of its leader, but when the leader acts in a cynical fashion, the team follows suit. Consequently, society gets saturated with bullshitters, excuse machines, malingerers, and crybabies. People detesting tow truck drives evince some combination of these four types of people. These people are the same buffoons who despise cops who pull them over for drunk driving and issue them a citation for a DUI saving some potential innocent person(s) from turning into victims of their dimwitted decision to drive while intoxicated. These people are the same buffoons who cheat on tests and plagiarize peoples, yet blame their teacher or professor for issuing them a flunking grade potentially leading to an expulsion. Rules and regulations are made for the purposes of adherence. If they are not enforced with stern repercussions for non-adherence, they simply get relegated to "guideline" status which nobody takes seriously. Ask the people who make the food pyramid guideline how many people take their "guidelines" seriously. Ask the Obamacare administrators if anyone is taking their measures seriously when they continue to delay the implementation of several facets of the health law germane to businesses in how they cover their employees. Basically, the fabric of American society continues to rapidly deteriorate because of an ersatz sense of entitlement permeating the psyche of Americans prompting them to believe the rules do not apply to them anymore. The lack of adherence to rules and the lack of an appropriate firm punishment to deter delinquent behavior coalesce to pin American society down an expedited track to complete maelstrom where we ostracize people (like tow truck drivers) who perform their job ingenuously while glorifying the miscreants (like Charlie Sheen, Justin Bieber, and Barack Obama) who continue to get rewarded for dastardly behavior. Honestly, Americans deserve incompetent leaders like the Double Bu-shits, Women Re-Clin(ed)-a-Ton, and Eating Crow-bama because all these crooks represent the blatantly ignorant, effete, vainglorious, pretentious and culturally vacuous populace that America has transformed into over the past few decades.

Here's a bonus way to identify you are a TAA since I want this book to serve as the definitive text to an ambitious prospective TAA 101 Course which would not be offered at Harvard or any other pretentious academic institution because it would require that people actually think for themselves. Certainly a course that encourages people to think beyond propagandistic dogma would be a novelty in America.

101. *You look like you just read an article on nuclear physics when someone mentions the term "halal" to you.* In case you neglected to notice (like you often do with your own children), Islam endured profound growth in America in the decade following 9/11 as the 2010 US Religion Census reported approximately 2.6 million people in America identifying them as Muslim. This evinces a profound increase from the 1 million Muslims reported in the same survey a decade earlier. Of course, the mathematically challenged TAA New York Daily reporter Meghan Neal reported it as a 67 percent increase when

in fact the increase is nearly 100 percent greater than that value. Apparently, she forgot that you need to take the difference between the final (2.6 million) and initial (1 million) values and divide it by the initial value (1 million) before multiplying by 100 to get the percentage change. Then again, since she does work for a liberal Islamophobic news source, one must wonder whether she deliberately fudged the numbers to palliate the perception of Islam's profound growth in America despite the liberal media's assiduous efforts to extirpate and vilify Muslims in every way, shape, or form. Either she is quantitatively inept or mendacious—a Venn diagram of these characteristics in Americans would indicate she has a nine in ten chance of being both. Anyway, I remain baffled at the fact most Americans still do not grasp the concept of "halal," yet the term "kosher" is utilized rather liberally in workaday language as well as in the popular media. I will give Americans credit for knowing the month of Ramadan as well as the fact that you utilize the term "Mecca"(also known as the holiest city in the Islamic faith) in a praiseful fashion. For example, I hear the term "cultural mecca" quite frequently to delineate a city with a resplendent cultural repertoire. However, Americans have still not come around to grasping the dietary laws pertaining to "halal" food. The worst part of the situation is the fact many restaurants owned by non-Muslims post their information on zabihah.com (a de facto halal registry for Muslims) claiming their food as "halal." However, when I walk into the restaurant confirming whether the food is halal, I receive a perplexed stare from the employees of the establishment. The employees call their manager and the manager simply relays the obvious fact they really lack the knowledge of the term "halal." A bit of advice to some of the owners who post on zabihah.com: if you are going to claim you serve halal food, you may want to edify your employees of this information so they do not get caught blindsided by a question they are not qualified to answer. American eating establishments have evolved considerably the last decade utilizing a bevy of codes catering to specific dietary preferences such as gluten free, vegan, vegetarian, organic, and kosher. When are these same establishments going to evolve into incorporating "halal" as part of their accommodating terminology? There are some chains such as Elevation Burger who have certified their burgers as halal much to my mirth as I ate at that place every week when I lived in Miami. Actually, I only ate there during their happy hour two for one burger specials since that represented the only time the burgers were not exorbitantly priced. However, the case of Elevation Burger (a national chain) demonstrates the ease to which the term "halal" can be implemented into the menus. The bottom line is Muslims evince a rapidly growing segment of society which will only continue to swell in the impending decades. Thus, it would behoove many of these restaurant chains and other food companies to start certifying certain products as halal, especially products that involve animal products, cultures and gelatin. Much of the time, an inquisitive Muslim must call the company's headquarters to obtain the information they need to determine whether they can lawfully eat the food according to Islamic dietary laws. Not only are the practicing Muslim's dietary choices severely restricted due to America's fascination with dousing pork and other meat onto all the food in the menu, but it is potentially further limited by the murky information pertaining to the superficially innocuous cheese products/enzymes. If America could lower its wings of humility to the grass-eating vegetarian hippies, the PETA banana nut bread vegans, the chapatti wearing Yahudis, and the nut-whacking, pizza hating glutton-free peeps, it is time to start including the halal-seeking magic carpet riding Muslims in the roundtable of food politics. By the way, if any American ever tried halal meat, they would wish all meat in America were made using the Islamic zabihah method since it's better tasting, healthier and more humane toward the animals. Otherwise, Americans continue to get fatter and more intellectually obtuse off eating cows fed meat, pigs squeezed like toothpaste, and abused chickens force fed cow manure. Then again, the ends certainly do justify the means, right Americans?

Glossary

All You Can EaTAA buffet: Where TAAs go to overindulge on salty foods and sugary drinks catalyzing their involuntary trip to the cardiologist surgery theatre for construction of a bypass, or two, or three.

Appe-TAA-zers: food items eaten by TAAs at restaurants so they do not have space to eat their large portioned entrees which they eventually throw away like spendthrift buffoons.

BAA: The black version of TAAs except they are more irritable, frugal, boisterous, cantankerous, and inimical. Basically, when you are around them, follow the same rules as if you are in a zoo with gorillas: do NOT pet them. If you want an easy method to spot BAAs, remember the nursery rhyme "Baa baa black sheep." This means two of the three blacks you see are BAAs while the other one is a black sheep.

BLT Sandwich: When one is surrounded by BAAs, LAAs, and TAAs in public choosing to mimic their activities since resistance is futile. Featured most prominently in "cosmopolitan" cities like Boston, Houston, New York City, Miami, and Los Angeles.

Food STAAmps: Program infested with TAAS, LAAs, and BAAs giving them public funds to buy more junk food (e.g. soda, chips, candy or cookies) or allowing them to swap the EBT cards to bankroll their alcohol, crack, cocaine, or heroin addictions.

Gin and TAAnic: Technique used by TAAs to get non-alcoholic drinkers drunk by making them think they are drinking a highly carbonated soda like ginger ale or Sprite when they are actually drinking a cocktail that will land them between someone's cock and tail later on during the night.

Hot Air Balloons: What TAA women carry around in their chest allowing them to float and spread their legs from bedroom to bedroom with ease along with providing them with the mileage to float to Mars if necessary.

Ins-TAA-gram: Where TAAs post tawdry selfies of themselves dressed in their panties, getting plastered with alcohol, putting on their makeup, fitting their condoms, and eating a hamburger amongst the displayed mundane activities for which they expect to receive gold stars on their Facebook and Twitter pages.

LAA: The Latino version of TAAs except they smell like spoiled chicken quesadillas, dress in public as if they are in a quinceanera version of "Groundhog Day," speak English as if they are auditioning for a part in the opera by stretching out every syllable, and act as though they still live in a third world country by refusing to follow standard rules and regulations.

Lizard TAA: TAAs who engage in PDAS by rolling out their tongues in red carpet form as if they are a walking zoo exhibit for how to play putt-putt golf with your mouth.

Mc TAAnolds: where 68 million TAAs eat daily even though they give it some of the lowest customer satisfaction ratings in the industry. I guess the obnoxious Happy Meal toys and the Playland where they can just unleash their children for a couple of hours explains America's fascination with it.

NaTAAlie Portman: A Jew and Harvard grad who needed a nose job to make it curve and point in a manner consistent with the snobbishness expected from the nefarious ivory tower intellectual coalition of the Poison Ivy Harvard Alumni Association and the AIPAC.

OuTAAback Steakhouse: Where TAAs go to spend $100 on gargantuan steaks and defibrillator deploying, waistline bulging, calorie bomb meals all under the guise of an exotic cultural experience since it involves exposure to a foreign language (Foster's).

PD-TAA: A swift way for TAAs to ascend into TAA-rific status by slurping each other like frisky lizards in public to shamelessly draw attention to themselves.

PhoTAAgraphy: A phenomena of Facebook in which TAAs deem it necessary to post photos of them boozing, smoking pot, posting selfies of themselves in their lingerie, guzzling down alcohol straight from a hose, participating in beer-pong tournaments, and tailgating.

PizTAA Hut: Company accounting for 14.8 percent of all pizza sales in the United States mostly because they slashed their prices commensurately with their dwindling quality. Of course, TAAs continue to eat there because enough of them are positioned across America to make even the meekest person blush. Ergo, resistance is futile.

Slot Machines: Procession lines of skimpily dressed TAArific tarts waiting for the next suitor to insert quarters through the front to unleash the jackpot from the backside. Best part about these slot machines is you don't need to visit Vegas to access them as they are probably lined up at a college campus near you.

STAArbucks: Where TAAs go to drink highly saccharine and superfluously caffeinated beverages in order to knowingly (and unknowingly) show their support for the Israeli army in their persistent and flagrant human rights violations against Palestinians along the Gaza Strip and West Bank. Keep drinking the blood coffee Americans.

TAAco Bell: Where TAAS go to eat cheap, pseudo-Mexican food to overcome intense hunger stemming from heavy alcoholic intake and a concomitant inebriated state which actually fools a person into thinking Taco Bell meat is edible.

TAA-flac: Company that utilizes a lame duck (literally) to attract TAAs who are stupid enough to buy insurance based on the word (literally one word) of the duck on television.

TAA-ilgating: What TAAs engage in several hours before a football game in order to get drunk before the game, paving the way to act like bacchanalian buffoons during the game while preparing them for the drinking games following the football game. Okay, I'm not going to lie: TAAs make some delicious food during those TAAgates (oops, I meant tailgates).

TAAmerica: The country with the highest concentration of TAAs in the entire world even though many more are flooding "Af Ghana stan and the I Rack"(in the words of Miss South Carolina from 2006) to speciously spread the doctrine of democracy.

TAA-nksgiving: A day where people are supposed to give thanks for their immense blessings only to get vitiated by TAAs who use it as an excuse to stuff their pie holes with more turkey, mashed potatoes, gravy, bread rolls, pecan pie, and stuffing in order to prepare themselves for the onslaught of "Black Friday" shopping the ensuing morning.

TAApplebees: Where drunk people go late night to take advantage of one-half off appetizers even if they have to deal with the most inept servers who take twenty minutes to start writing your order, argue with you about stale chips and burnt food, and check on you every half an hour for water refills. If they are your "neighborhood restaurant," perhaps you should consider leaving because the hoodlums are taking over.

TAArific: someone who is terrific at being a TAA.

TAA training: the sine qua non of all American training. Before they learn how to crawl, walk, use a toilet, or count, they learn the etiquettes of being spoiled, abrasive, entitled, philistine brats.

TAA-Witter: Where TAAs go to sound off and make inappropriate comments about crackers, spics, niggers, coons, kaiks, fags, legal cases, tragedies, and indignation issuing banal apologies after getting reprimanded, fired from their job, or kicked off a team because they actually mistook the Freedom of Speech for Freedom to Act Like an Idiot Without Consequences.

TAA-ylor Swift: The most overrated singer in America whose songs evince little but pastiches and clichéd dialogue while her love interests in real life seem to shuffle as rapidly as the head coaches for the Cleveland Browns. Quite fitting since they both suck lots of dick. She should have starred in a movie called Easter rather than Valentine's Day because she really knows how to lay eggs on the screen with her putrid acting.

Ti-TAA-nic: A movie TAAs think of as a timeless love story when it is just another excuse for gals to salivate over Leo DiCaprio while prurient guys salivate over the bedroom action following the three hours of torture.

Wal-MarTAA: Where TAAs shop for their food, clothing, bicycles, Hallmark cards, electronics, Taylor Swift calendars, and Michigan Wolverine jerseys in order to save money without any concern for the human rights violations they commit against their workers simply due to the fact they do not view their workers as human.

WCW: Abbreviation for white crack whores who happen to be the most numerous class of female TAAs characterized by the delusional appraisal of their own promiscuous, sullen, drug-induced behavior construed as advancement of women's rights. It can also be abbreviated as White Coke Whores since many women prefer cocaine to crack even though they probably are not lucid enough to discern between the two.

www.ingramcontent.com/pod-product-compliance
Lightning Source LLC
Chambersburg PA
CBHW020532290526
45786CB00002B/842